| DATE DUE | | | |
|---|---|---|---|
|  |  |  |  |
|  |  |  |  |
|  |  |  |  |
|  |  |  |  |
|  |  |  |  |
|  |  |  |  |
|  |  |  |  |
|  |  |  |  |
|  |  |  |  |
|  |  |  |  |
|  |  |  |  |
|  |  |  |  |

# Vida Dutton Scudder

## Twayne's United States Authors Series

Kenneth Eble, Editor

*University of Utah*

TUSAS 421

VIDA DUTTON SCUDDER
(1861–1954)
Photograph courtesy of
Wellesley College

# Vida Dutton Scudder

## By Theresa Corcoran, S.C.

*Mount Saint Vincent University*
*Halifax, Nova Scotia*

*Twayne Publishers* • *Boston*

*Vida Dutton Scudder*

Theresa Corcoran, S.C.

Book Production by Marne B. Sultz
Book Design by Barbara Anderson


Printed on permanent/durable
acid-free paper and bound in
The United States of America.




Library of Congress Cataloging in Publication Data

Corcoran, Theresa.
    Vida Dutton Scudder.

    (Twayne's United States authors series; TUSAS 421)
    Bibliography: p. 126
    Includes Index
    1. Scudder, Vida Dutton, 1861–1954—Criticism and
interpretation. 1. Title. II. Series.
PS3537.C975Z63        818'.4'09        82–3095
ISBN 0–8057–7354–1                    AACR2

*For all my sisters*

# Contents

## About the Author

Theresa Corcoran, S.C., is an associate professor of history at Mount Saint Vincent University, Halifax, Nova Scotia. Born and educated in Boston she received a B.A. in English from Emmanuel College, Boston, an M.A. in European history from Villanova University, and a Ph.D. in United States history from Georgetown University. After joining the Congregation of the Sisters of Charity she taught school in Nova Scotia and in Boston. Since 1965 she has been on the faculty at Mount Saint Vincent University where she has served as chairperson of the department of history and of the division of history, philosophy, political studies and religious studies. She teaches courses in United States history, women's history, and the history of childhood and has published in various scholarly journals.

# *Preface*

Vida Dutton Scudder's long life (1861–1954) spanned the two major reform periods of modern America. As teacher, writer, reformer, Scudder was in the vanguard of the many diverse movements in the country looking toward a new society. Historians seldom fail to mention her work in the settlements, with the immigrants, with the women's labor unions in Boston, with the early Christian Socialist groups in the United States, but little more is said. No detailed study of her life and work or of the impact of her thinking on the social ferment of the time has ever been published. Arthur Mann in *Yankee Reformers in an Urban Age* (1954) devoted one section of his chapter "The New and Newer Women as Reformers" to Vida Dutton Scudder, and he was fortunate enough to have talked with her and to have used her personal papers. Since then those papers have been lost or destroyed.

Other historians have singled out Scudder as part of a larger study. William L. O'Neill in *Everyone Was Brave* (1969) considered her traditional Bostonian private life, highly successful professional career, and radical socialist views as a necessary part of the total picture of the feminist movement in the early twentieth century. Though Scudder hated segregated discussions of women as women, her long career was directed chiefly to advancing the position of women. The emotional stresses of the new breed of women emerging at the turn of the century were a large part of her own lifelong quest for "reality," and a closer look at her writings reveals her personal response to the social, economic, emotional, and spiritual crises experienced by so many of that first generation of college-educated women. No one has written more eloquently or sincerely of the value of real friendship among women than Scudder herself for whom friendship was a special art and virtue.

Jessie Bernard in *Academic Women* (1964) recalled the impact of Vida Scudder on her own generation of college women. Scudder saw her career as teacher of English Literature at Wellesley College for over forty years as a vital part of her mission to her own class. The tensions between her academic life and her wider community involvement were often at the breaking point, and had Scudder devoted her energies entirely to the one or the other her name would be as familiar today as that of Katherine Lee Bates or Jane Addams. But Scudder was more the intellectual than the academic or the activist. Her mind darted in so many directions that even her high-strung body could not always keep pace. This intense intellectual energy fed on a deep Christian faith and directed Scudder to a more radical view of Christianity and of the importance of the church in industrial society. Most studies of the reform impulses within the churches mention Scudder as one of the core members of these reform groups. The renewed interest of historians in the role of women in the church and in radical societies should reveal more of Scudder's role and influence in these areas. Peter Fredericks's article on Scudder in *The New England Quarterly* (1970) and my two articles in the *Anglican Theological Review* (1975) and in the *Essex Institute Historical Collections* (1979) have attempted to do this.

Overall, Scudder's greatest contribution has been to the growth of religious social thought in America. Because of the length and breadth of Scudder's career as a writer I have limited myself to the development of her Christian social thought as seen in her major published books. Many of these ideas were first tested out in articles in a variety of journals. Only when necessary to round out or show a change in her thinking are these articles discussed in detail. Scudder realized that her three-pronged career as teacher, writer, reformer would detract from her power as a writer. This was a sacrifice she made in the ardor of youth but which she neither regretted nor reneged on. At times one aspect of this career predominates in her writing. Here I have approached her work chronologically as much as possible while trying to show some unifying theme. In Chapter 2, for example, I deal with books of literary criticism because in the early years of her academic career the ambition to write vied strongly with the demand for personal experience. In Chapter 3 the tensions of her life are revealed and then resolved by her intimacy with the Italian saints. Chapter 4 is largely a detailed analysis of her *Socialism and Character* which, years later, she still felt contained some of her best thinking. Here Scudder anticipated the Christian-Marxist dialogue of the mid-twentieth century. In Chapter 5, Scudder is the convinced Christian Socialist urging fellow Christians to realize the power inherent in their faith. Chapter 6 discusses her major work *The Franciscan Adventure* which established her as one of the foremost Franciscan scholars in the United States as well as a leading churchwoman and revolutionary. In Chapter 7 I look at Scudder's autobiography and then her biographical study of Father James Huntington. Chapter 8 considers her changing ideas on pacifism and feminism and a brief conclusion assesses her place in American life and thought. The introductory chapter relies heavily on her own autobiography for details of her life since the manuscript sources are so slim. Some of these incidents I have enlarged on, where possible, in later chapters to provide necessary background for the works discussed, keeping in mind that this is the first full-length study of Vida Scudder. Because the message is all-important to Scudder, the study will be more contextual analysis than literary criticism for overall her writing is more journalistic than belles-lettres and her attempt to fashion a Christian Socialist mentality in the churches and in society requires more exposition than critique.

In the absence of manuscript sources and even of secondary material, Vida Scudder introduced me to many people whose help and interest have been essential and encouraging. When I first began my study, Peter Oliver, then at the Harvard-Andover library, shared his Scudder bibliography with me, saving me many hours of research. I was indeed fortunate to meet Mercy Gerrior, of Gorham, New Hampshire, housekeeper for Vida Scudder for over forty years; she spoke intimately to me about both Scudder and her friend Florence Converse. Mercy Gerrior put me in contact with members of the Society of the Companions of the Holy Cross who welcomed me to Adelynrood, their summer home in Byfield,

Massachusetts, spoke frankly to me about their memories of Miss Scudder, and allowed me to use whatever Scudder materials I could find. Winifred Hulbert, S.C.H.C., has been friend and resource person over the years. Their archivist Ruth Leonard, S.C.H.C., has been especially helpful. So also was Wilma Slaight, archivist at Wellesley College. The Reverend Joseph F. Fletcher of Episcopal Theological School, Cambridge, in a long interview made me aware of the impact of the revolutionary Scudder on the young clergymen of his day and of their devotion to and admiration for "Aunt Vida." Many others forwarded letters and wrote me of their recollections of Scudder. All of these have helped to fill out the picture that the printed page had sketched.

The literary heirs of Vida Dutton Scudder are hard to determine definitively. I am grateful to the following who, in so far as they were able, permitted me to quote from Scudder material in their collections: The Wellesley College Archives, the Sophia Smith Collection, and the Houghton Library for the use of Horace Scudder materials. My thanks to the Swarthmore College Peace Collection for permission to quote from Scudder letters in The Jane Addams Papers, to the American Baptist Historical Society, Rochester, New York, for materials in Dores R. Sharpe Collection of Walter Rauschenbusch Papers. A special thank you to Joseph F. Fletcher for use of quotations from *Christianity and Property* and to William Bross Lloyd, Jr., for permission to use Henry Lloyd letters in Wellesley College Archives and to quote from Caro Lloyd's *Henry Demarest Lloyd: A Biography*.

For copyright permission I am indebted to J. M. Dent and Sons, London, England, and E. P. Dutton Company of New York for use of quotations from books written by Vida Dutton Scudder.

Theresa Corcoran, S.C.

*Mount Saint Vincent University*

# Chronology

1861    Born in Madura, India, December 15, Julia Davida, the only daughter of David Coit Scudder, a Congregationalist missionary, and Harriet Dutton Scudder.

1862    After the death of her husband Harriet Scudder returned with her infant daughter to her parental home in Auburndale, Massachusetts.

1862–1877    Vida Scudder grew up in Auburndale and Boston, attended private schools, and travelled extensively in Europe with her mother and aunt, Julia Dutton.

1878    Enrolled in first class of Girls' Latin School, Boston.

1880–1884    Attended Smith College. Wrote a playlet *Mitsu-Yu Nissi* (1888) and several short stories and articles published under the pseudonym Davida Coit.

1884    Postgraduate study in literature at Oxford. Attended the last lectures of John Ruskin at Oxford.

1885    Travelled in Europe with her mother before returning to Boston. "The Poetic Element in Medieval Art" published in the *Atlantic Monthly.*

1886–1887    Earned M.A. from Smith College. Joined Bellamy's Nationalist Club in Boston. Met William D. P. Bliss and became a charter member of his Christian Socialist groups.

1887    Edited *George MacDonald: Poems* (with Clara French). *The Grotesque in Gothic Art,* based on work done at Oxford, published as a pamphlet. Her M.A. thesis published as a two-part essay "The Effect of the Scientific Temper on Modern Poetry" in the *Andover Review.* Joined faculty of English Literature at Wellesley College. Initiated plans for a college settlement.

1889 Joined the Society of the Companions of the Holy Cross, a lifelong commitment for Scudder. College Settlement at Rivington Street in New York City opened. Edited Macaulay's *Essay on Lord Clive.*

1890 Edited *An Introduction to the Writings of John Ruskin.* College Settlements Association formed with Vida Scudder as secretary of the Electoral Board.

1892 Philadelphia College Settlement opened.

1893–1895 Took a two-year leave of absence from Wellesley. Spent first year with Helena S. Dudley, Headworker at Denison House, Boston, in official opening of the settlement and the following year studying at the Sorbonne.

1895 *The Witness of Denial* and *The Life of the Spirit in the Modern English Poets* published.

1898 *Social Ideals in English Letters* published.

1900 Involved in controversy over the Rockefeller gift to Wellesley College.

1901–1903 Severe illness as result of strains of social concerns and academic life. Recuperated in Italy where interest in Italian saints and medieval literature developed. First novel, *A Listener in Babel,* published.

1904 Organized the Circolo Italo-Americano, a group of well-educated Italians and Americans, to work with Italian immigrants. An Italian Club formed at Denison House.

1905 *Saint Catherine of Siena as Seen in Her Letters* published.

1907 *The Disciple of a Saint,* a novel, published.

1910 Edited *The Ecclesiastical History of the English Nation* and *The Journal with Other Writings of John Woolman* for Everyman's Library.

1911 Joined Socialist Party. Vice-president of the Church Socialist League organized by Bishop Bernard I. Bell.

1912    *Socialism and Character* published. Resigned from active work in Denison House because of her socialist views. Scudder and her mother moved to Wellesley. Her speech to women during the Lawrence textile strike sparked controversy.

1913–1915    Appointed to new Joint Commission of Social Service in Episcopal Church. Vice-president of the Intercollegiate Socialist Society. Spoke at Ford Hall Forum on "Moral Assets of Class Struggle." Addressed the Intercollegiate Socialist Society's Labor Day Week-End Conference on "The Ethics of Socialism."

1916    "The Alleged Failure of the Church to Meet the Social Emergency," an address to Thirty-third Church Congress of Protestant Episcopal Church.

1917    *Le Morte d'Arthur of Sir Thomas Malory and Its Sources* and *The Church and the Hour: Reflections of a Socialist Churchwoman* published.

1918    Lectured at Cambridge Conference on "Social Teachings of the Christian Year."

1919    Founding member of Church League for Industrial Democracy. Resigned from Denison House Board of Directors because of opposition to her radicalism. Florence Converse and her mother came to live with Scudders.

1920    Death of mother, Harriet Scudder, in January.

1921–1922    Sabbatical leave spent in Italy studying Saint Francis and his followers. Honorary degree from Wellesley College. *The Social Teachings of the Christian Year* published.

1922    Honorary degree from Smith College.

1927    *Brother John,* a novel, published.

1928    Retired from Wellesley College. Research in Italy.

1930–1932    Dean of Summer School of Christian Social Ethics held on Wellesley campus.

1931   Lectured weekly at New School of Social Research in New York City. *The Franciscan Adventure* published.

1933   Organized with Professor Edwin Booth of Boston University The Institute of Franciscan Studies sponsored by the Society of the Companions of the Holy Cross at Adelynrood, South Byfield, Massachusetts.

1937   Her autobiography, *On Journey,* published.

1938   "Conflicting Loyalties" in *Radical Religion.*

1939   *The Privilege of Age* published.

1940   *Father Huntington, Founder of the Order of the Holy Cross* published.

1942   Honorary Doctor of Divinity from Nashota House, in Wisconsin, the first woman to receive an honorary degree from a school of divinity.

1944   Organized conference on The Church's Responsibility Toward Racial Groups held at Adelynrood, South Byfield, Massachusetts. Edited *Letters to Her Companions* by Emily Malbone Morgan, foundress of the Society of the Companions of the Holy Cross.

1947   Wrote "Anglican Thought on Property" in *Christianity and Property,* edited by Joseph F. Fletcher. Book is dedicated to Vida Scudder in recognition of her great contribution to Christian social thought.

1952   *My Quest for Reality,* a sequel to her autobiography, published.

1954   Died October 9, age 93, in her Wellesley home. Her body was cremated and interred in Mt. Auburn Cemetery, Cambridge, Massachusetts.

## Chapter One

# Life's Terrible Choices

It was early in November, 1897, when Vida Dutton Scudder completed her *Social Ideals in English Letters*. She paused to consider seriously the criticism of a good friend and colleague at Wellesley College that her social involvement was endangering her literary career. Finally and deliberately she replied in words that would describe and sum up her life. "I must live if I am to interpret life. I cannot shut myself away and study medieval legends of the Holy Grail while men are perishing for the Bread of Life. No! I will work for my own generation; I will help the immediate need; I will abandon dreams of work that shall endure." For the past ten years Vida Scudder, an outstanding teacher and promising scholar, had been on the faculty at Wellesley, but teaching and writing had to compete with social and community interests far removed from Wellesley. Shortly after coming to the college she had organized the college settlements in New York, Philadelphia, and Boston. About the same time she had joined a Christian Socialist group in Boston and even now was a leading figure in similar groups both within and outside the Episcopal Church. Both of these interests had involved her in the labor movement in Boston. The strain of working at such different levels was evident to her friend, if not to Vida, whose lengthy reply revealed a commitment to social justice that overcame literary ambition. "There must be people for their decade, as well as people for all time," she wrote. "I will give myself where I can be of modest, immediate use; and if this is a queer new way of burying my small talent . . . why, somehow I have not much fear of the outer darkness; for there is a Presence that once known can never be lost."[1]

Vida Scudder's need to live life to its fullest stemmed from a haunting sense of unreality that plagued her early years and from a constant fret of privilege unshared that persisted for a lifetime. Neither is hard to trace.

## The Formative Years

Julia Davida Scudder was born in Madura, India, December 15, 1861, the only child of David Coit Scudder, a Congregationalist missionary and Harriet Dutton Scudder. During his first year in India David Scudder drowned, and Harriet Scudder returned with her daughter to her parents' home in Auburndale, Massachusetts. Both Scudders and Duttons were old New England families, and Vida, a delicate, sensitive child, grew up surrounded by doting grandparents, distinguished aunts and uncles, and a devoted mother.[2] Her grandparents, Charles and Sarah Lathrop (Coit) Scudder, were known for an eagerness to serve, and their Boston home was always open to missionaries preparing for or returning from the mission fields. Charles Scudder had three sons in this third marriage. Samuel was an entomologist and president of the Boston Association of Natural History. Horace was a distinguished author, editor of the *Atlantic Monthly,* and literary advisor to Houghton-Mifflin Company. The eldest son, David, Vida's father, determined on a missionary career while at Williams College and devoted himself unsparingly to preparation for his life in India. Besides mastering the languages of the provinces to which he was assigned, David steeped himself in oriental philosophies. His one fear was of intellectual stagnation, and he prepared against it methodically. These intense intellectual energies combined with zeal and compassion for human need and a deep interior life were David Scudder's greatest legacy to his only child.[3]

The Dutton side of the family was not so numerous but more familiar to Vida in her youth. For her first six years the Dutton grandparents, Aunt Julia Dutton (a nurse and later a doctor), and Harriet Scudder with Vida made their home together. Her dearest uncle, Horace Dutton, a frequent visitor, spent the happiest years of his life in city mission work. Another uncle, Edward, was head of the publishing firm of E. P. Dutton in New York. Undoubtedly her mother, Harriet Scudder, had the greatest influence on Vida. Shortly after her grandparents' death the Auburndale home was sold, and Vida spent the following three years travelling in Europe with her mother and Aunt Julia. Here the precocious, impressionable child wandering about the ancient ruins, medieval cathedrals, and modern museums, absorbed her mother's devotion to beauty and to tradition; these were to be the hallmarks of her own life.

Vida was ten when the travellers returned from Europe. She had never been to school in Boston, and the experience at Miss Sanger's private school was not a happy one. Her natural shyness with people grew in alarming proportions in the next few years. Vida's active mind was aware of the religious excitement in Boston in the 1870s, and she took part in the religious discussions in the family which preceded her mother's decision to join the Episcopal Church.

By 1875 Vida was graduated from Miss Sanger's school, and, following her mother's example, she was confirmed by Phillips Brooks in the Protestant Episcopal Church. Then the three, Vida, Harriet Scudder, and Aunt Julia, returned to Europe. During the next year and a half Vida grew into a young lady and became aware of herself at last as an "integrated personality."[4] Though she was still troubled by a sense of unreality in her own life during these years and for many years after, Vida was a much more normal girl when she returned to Boston in 1877. In 1878 she entered the first class of Girls' Latin School where the discipline of fixed study and scholarly precision was a new and valuable experience. Four years at Smith College followed, next best to the young girl's dream of enrolling at Harvard disguised as a boy. Smith offered little intellectual challenge but it was Vida's gentle introduction to real life. For the first and only time she was separated from her mother and forced to rely on her own resources. More important, Vida Scudder learned the need and importance of group relationships and later wrote often of the "permanent enrichment of life" in these college friendships.[5] Her career as a writer also took shape in these years. Several short stories appeared under a pseudonym, Davida Coit. A playlet, *Mitsu-Yu Nissi*, written with a classmate, Frona Brooks, was produced at Smith and published in pamphlet form in 1888. Illness in her senior year, diagnosed as curvature of the spine, confined her to bed, but two essays written in place of regular class work were published: "Immortality and Evolution" in the *New Englander* in 1884 and "The Moral Dangers of Musical Devotees" in the *Andover Review* in 1887.[6]

In the fall of 1884 Vida Scudder sailed for England, accompanied by her mother and Clara French, her close friend. There she did graduate study in English at Oxford; the highlight of those Oxford days was the opportunity to attend the last lectures of John Ruskin. Scudder came away with a social radicalism that grew in intensity. Her lifetime would be spent in seeking answers to some of the questions that arose during those lectures. Her immediate response, however, was to join the Salvation Army in an effort to blunt the "intolerable stabbing pain," as she realized for the first time the "plethora of privilege" surrounding her. When Vida Scudder returned to Boston in 1885, she discovered that despite her advanced education a middle-class girl of means was still expected to be a passive spectator. She dabbled in art, earned an M.A. from Smith, but her writing was frustrated. What does one write if idealism has nothing but dreams and abstractions to play on? Again, fears of unreality, of living always at second hand, attacked her.[7]

## The Wellesley Years

Brooding, groping, bored, Vida Scudder finally accepted a position in the English department at Wellesley College in 1887. For the next forty-one years Wellesley remained the focal point of her activity. The women's colleges were new and exciting in the 1880s, and Vida Scudder threw herself into her work with an intensity that recalls her father's preparation for his life work. Teaching gave her a needed self-confidence, and the shyness that had dogged all her days remarkably disappeared as she faced her first class. But still there were doubts. In a few months she had fitted together a plan that would combine her love of teaching and her desire to work for the poor with her sense of mission to her own class. Her plan for a settlement house went awry at first, but in 1889 the first college settlement opened on Rivington Street in New York City, antedating by a few weeks the now-famous Hull House. At this time Scudder was committed to Wellesley by a three-year contract, but she spent the Christmas holidays in the settlement that year, and for the first time her life "was unshadowed by a grey tinge of remorse."[8]

The college settlements were only one phase of the larger settlement movement sweeping the country in the 1890s, and in the summer of 1892 pioneers in these settlements met at Plymouth, Massachusetts. In her presentation Scudder acknowledged the truth of many of the criticisms of the settlements: their lack of professionalism, their amateur character; but to her these were their chief value. The young men and women in the settlements were demanding "not improvement in method but regeneration in life and for such regeneration a settlement stands."[9]

By this time a second college settlement house had opened in Philadelphia, and Vida Scudder spent six weeks there. In 1893 Scudder took a two-year leave of absence from Wellesley to join the Headworker Helena S. Dudley in the official opening of Denison House on Tyler Street in Boston's South End. The settlement met a real challenge in the economic depression of that year. Both Scudder and Dudley realized the importance of unionization for the women workers in the neighborhood and invited Mary Kenney O'Sullivan from Hull House to spearhead that work. That winter Scudder and Helena Dudley were elected delegates to the Central Labor Union and learned of the class struggle firsthand. The second year of her leave Scudder spent studying at the Sorbonne. Whether these were years of decision for her or not is uncertain. Perhaps the family claim or academic pull was stronger. Or she may have recognized that her talents could be used better in promotional work on the college campuses. For the next twenty years, while still teaching at Wellesley, Scudder was the prime mover at Denison House, supplying the "ideas" while Helena Dudley supplied the "human warmth and contacts."[10]

In another way, too, 1887 was a pivotal year for Vida Scudder. In the trying months after her return from Oxford Scudder had gone with her uncle Horace Dutton to meetings of Bellamy's Nationalist Clubs where she met William Dwight Porter Bliss. Both were impatient with the secular and passive tone of these meetings, and in 1889 Scudder became one of the charter members of Bliss's Christian Socialist Society. In the next few years the members of this society became the nucleus of a small congregation in the Episcopal Church, the Church of the Carpenter. A supplementary group, the Brotherhood of the Carpenter, aimed to bring together men and women of all persuasions to discuss the application of Christianity to social problems. Here Scudder met labor leaders like George McNeill and Harry Lloyd and discussed the practical needs of the workers in the light of the more utopian ideals of the Christian commonwealth. Ideas and contacts that began here were to prove invaluable in her work at Denison House. Scudder contributed often to *The Dawn,* the newspaper of the society, and in pamphlets written for the Christian Social Union in the next decade she had an opportunity to formulate and clarify her own socialist ideas. This tiny movement for social justice within the Episcopal Church became her consuming interest in the years ahead, deepening her own faith and her commitment to socialism.[11]

But these three areas of interest—teaching, settlement work, and Christian Socialism—competed with her ambition to make a name for herself in letters. Besides numerous articles in religious and scholarly journals Scudder published *The Witness of Denial* (1895), *The Life of the Spirit in the Modern English Poets* (1895), and *Social Ideals in English Letters* (1898), which show the close bond between her literary interests and her social concern. All these interests gave new intensity to her teaching, and Scudder's influence spread beyond the Wellesley campus. Jessie Bernard in *Academic Women* recalled her friend's description of her Wellesley teacher, "When you touch her, sparks fly," and her banker-father's comment that he would "never send another daughter of his to Wellesley to be inflamed by those sparks."[12] More than once Scudder was told that she was a detriment to the college, but it was her outspoken opposition to a Rockefeller gift to the college that led to her direct disagreement with the administration and trustees in 1900. Outraged by the offer, Scudder, the gadfly of the faculty conscience, led a protest among faculty and students against accepting "tainted money." Her uncle, Horace Scudder, himself a trustee, tempered her letters to the Board of Trustees and cautioned her about resigning precipitately. Persuaded by her spiritual director, the Reverend Charles Brent, rector of St. Stephen's Church in Boston, and by other reformers such as Henry D. Lloyd, that the loss of the radicals would be disastrous for the colleges Scudder stayed on, and the college accepted the gift and subsequent large endowments. Still Scudder constantly reproached herself for the many personal adjustments or compromises she was forced to make in following her career. In 1901 her health broke under the mental and physical strain. Her illness, diagnosed as complete exhaustion, forced her to suspend all activities for the next two years. Accompanied by her mother who was always puzzled and distressed by her daughter's radicalism, and by Florence Converse, a former student and close friend, she sailed for Europe. In Italy her interest in the medieval, which went back to her youth and her Oxford days, brought her into contact with the Italian saints. The letters of Saint Catherine of Siena were a needed balm for her troubled soul and in the years ahead led her to a new literary interest as well as to new work with the Italian immigrants at Denison House and with the Circolo Italo-Americano which she organized to help in this work.[13]

## Christian Socialism

For many years Vida Scudder had referred to herself as an avowed socialist. By the 1900s she had become more politically oriented; however, it was not until 1911 that she was able to reconcile the conflicts between Christianity and socialism sufficiently to join the Socialist Party. Here she identified with the conservative or non-violent wing of the Party; her book *Socialism and Character* reveals her socialist thinking at the time. Scudder was convinced that it was important for Christians committed to socialism to make their views heard in the Party, and she tried with little success to bring other church leaders and reformers to the Party. It was equally important for radical voices to speak out in the churches, so in 1911 she joined the Episcopal Church Socialist League, a church group of orthodox socialists who hoped to bring Christians to apply the teachings of Christ to industrial and social relations.[14]

Through her socialist connections Scudder was asked to speak in Lawrence, Massachusetts, during the great textile strike of 1912. By this time Lawrence had attracted nationwide attention, and the speeches of Vida Scudder and her Wellesley colleague, Ellen Hayes, were reprinted in papers throughout the country. The *Boston Evening Transcript* denounced both of them for spreading radical doctrine and called for their resignations. In a letter to Ellen Pendleton, President of Wellesley College, Scudder explained her socialist position but disavowed any connection with the International Workers of the World. Though not asked to resign, she was required to suspend for the next year the course for which she had become famous at Wellesley, "Social Ideals in English Letters."[15]

In May of 1912, realizing that she was too radical for the present committee, Scudder resigned her active role at Denison House, and in the fall she and her mother moved from Boston to their new home in Wellesley. She looked forward to a more active role in the life of the college community and was more convinced than ever that the colleges needed the radicals. She joined the newly reorganized Intercollegiate Socialist Society and was in great demand as a lecturer on New England college campuses. It was a similar educational role that Scudder envisioned for herself in the Society of the Companions of the Holy Cross, a group of women of the Anglican communion united in a spiritual companionship and dedicated to intercessory prayer for social justice and church unity. There were over forty members in the Society when Scudder joined in 1889, but so great was her influence that she is usually considered one of the founders and credited with broadening the vision of the Society. Largely through Vida Scudder, many women involved in active social work joined the Society and like Scudder found here a needed support for their daily work and their spiritual lives as well. In the early twentieth century the Society worked at many levels to alert the Episcopal Church to its social responsibilities.[16]

For the first time Vida Scudder sensed some unity in her life and work. Then war in Europe shattered the hopes of reformers and radicals in the United States. Immersed as she was in her study of *Le Morte d'Arthur*, Scudder's "apologia for war was contained in one word: chivalry." Though she was dismayed by the rhetoric of the war and looked upon the philosophy of preparedness as a "philosophy of fear," she supported President Wilson's decision for war in 1917. Still, the war years were a particularly lonely period. The friends she valued most had never accepted her socialist views. Now she was unable to accept their absolute pacifism. Even her radical socialist friends found it difficult to agree with her view that pacifism was a disavowal of the class war. However, she was so outspoken in her defense of the pacifist's right to dissent that she often had to defend herself against charges of pacifism.[17] By 1923 the Fellowship of Reconciliation recognized that true peace demanded a drastic reorganization of society; Vida Scudder was ready to join that group. That year she also lectured at the summer school of the Women's International League for Peace and Freedom meeting near Prague. By the 1930s she was an absolute pacifist, giving pacifism precedence over economic reform or social welfare, a position she maintained for the rest of her life.[18]

The war had a divisive effect on the Church Socialist League, too, and Scudder, anxious to keep that tiny spark of radicalism alive in the church, organized the Church League for Industrial Democracy as a means of uniting radical and liberal Christians committed to the cause of social justice but wary of supporting any one political creed. Throughout the 1920s CLID was the leading radical church group and attracted many former members of the Church Socialist League, which still suffered from wartime divi-

sions. Scudder was thus the link between these two phases of
Christian Socialism in the Episcopal Church.[19]

The colleges, too, came under attack in the twenties, and Wellesley was no exception. Scudder had been active also in reorganizing
the Intercollegiate Socialist Society into the League for Industrial
Democracy and at this time began her lasting friendship with Norman Thomas. As a member of the American Civil Liberties Union
she was a prime target of reactionary critics in postwar years. When
in 1921 Calvin Coolidge attacked the women's colleges as "hotbeds
of radicalism," the students at Wellesley came to the defense of the
faculty, proud to be in an institution where people like Vida
Scudder still carried on "her 'demoralizing and destructive work'
of seeking to make a modern fact of Christ's teaching of the brotherhood of man."[20]

But Scudder herself felt "pretty passive" in the immediate postwar decade, though not discouraged. She was glad when a sabbatical leave in 1922 gave her the opportunity to steep herself
for a time in her Franciscan studies. In January of 1920 her mother
had died, and although Harriet Scudder had been living con-
tentedly "in heavenly places" for a few years before, the final
separation was still difficult. Fortunately, Florence Converse and
her mother had joined the Scudder household in 1919, and she
appreciated their love and companionship. Early in the 1920s her
friends Lucy Smith and Helena Dudley also came to live with her,
and Scudder delighted in her "companion house."[21]

After her retirement from the college in 1928 Scudder dedicated
herself unreservedly to stern scholarly research and writing. *The
Franciscan Adventure* (1931) established her as a foremost Franciscan scholar. Still she continued to explore every path that might
lead to social redemption. The industrial democracy she had hoped
for did not emerge, and though she delighted in being called a
communist, she had long since outgrown her Marxian concepts.
Her interest in the Russian experience continued, but she realized
that unless a revolution proceeded from a Christian concept of
humanity it could offer no solution to social ills. Inspired by the
new Anglo-Catholic movement in the Church of England, Scudder

helped to organize, and for the first three years was Dean of the Summer School of Christian Social Ethics which opened on the Wellesley College campus in 1930 under the auspices of the Church League for Industrial Democracy. In this way she directed another generation of church leaders not into the settlements or slums but into the "jungle of social theories" which was the modern challenge. In 1931, almost 70, she journeyed weekly to lecture in the New School of Social Research in New York.[22] At the summer home of the Society of the Companions of the Holy Cross in South Byfield, Massachusetts, she convened institutes and workshops on Saint Francis and Today, Peace, The Labor Movement, and the Churches' Responsibility toward Racial Groups, thus keeping church leaders and the members of the Society in touch with the crucial social issues and with radical Christian thought. Though age curtailed her activity, through her writing and lecturing "Aunt Vida" continued to inspire, direct, and encourage new leaders in the church. In 1942 Nashota House in Wisconsin awarded her an honorary degree, the first woman ever to be so honored by a divinity school. In 1945 she lectured on "Anglican Thought on Property," at the conference on Christian Social Teachings at the Episcopal Theological School in Cambridge. When the papers were published the following year, the contributors, all leading churchmen and theologians, agreed that there was "no other person in the American scene to whom a book on Christianity and property could so rightly be dedicated."[23] In 1950, crippled with age and almost stone deaf, Scudder began her last book, *My Quest for Reality,* a sequel to her autobiography which revealed a mind still very much attuned to the world in which she lived. Professor Douglas V. Steere of Haverford College recalled his last visit with Vida Scudder in these years. With a familiar searching look, she cocked her head and remarked, "Professor Steere, I am all packed and ready to go. But I just can't bear to leave. It's all so interesting."[24] She died suddenly in her home on October 9, 1954. The long quest for reality, which she recognized as the search for God and her greatest privilege to share, was over.

## Chapter Two

# Emergence as a Literary Critic

When Vida Scudder began teaching at Wellesley College in 1887, the intellectual paralysis that had gripped her since her return from Europe suddenly disappeared. With the feverish preparation for her classes came an irrepressible desire to write. In the next few years articles and short stories appeared in a variety of journals, *Poet Lore,* the *Atlantic Monthly,* the *Andover Review,* among others. In addition, she prepared study guides and wrote lengthy introductions for student editions of such classics as *Macaulay's Essay on Lord Clive* and an *Introduction to the Writings of John Ruskin.*[1] By this time she had become the natural literary spokesperson for the numerous Christian Socialist groups that she had joined and an active member in such civic clubs as the Boston Authors' Club, the Boston Browning Society, and the Twentieth Century Club. As secretary to the Electoral Board of the College Settlements Association, she promoted that work on college campuses. The intellectual stimulus in the Wellesley College English department presented a special challenge, and Scudder was determined to make her contribution to American letters. An immensely popular teacher and lecturer, Scudder published in 1895 an abridgment of a series of lectures on modern English prose writers, *The Witness of Denial,* which indicates the direction her major literary efforts were to take in these years. In these lectures she reviewed the currents of agnosticism in the nineteenth-century prose masters to show their positive contributions to faith.[2]

Scudder saw agnosticism moving through three stages which she discussed under the headings of the religion of mystery, the religion of humanity, and the religion of morality. Each of these phases of denial was a struggle for freedom, which, unfortunately, the Church in England met by appeals to authority rather than by reliance on its own inner resources. Such appeals were of little avail. By the end of the century the waves of agnosticism had played themselves out. When men again sought the spiritual and turned at last to the church, they were led not by tradition or authority but by individual struggle and personal prayer. In the process these agnostics had freed the church from its dependence on authority and prestige and prepared it for a new challenge. The spiritual renewal she saw in the church at the end of the century came at a time of severe crisis in the industrial sphere. Here was the church's new opportunity to command allegiance, to exert leadership not by claims to authority but by a revelation of the life within (149–52).

These lectures had a tremendous impact, for, in addition to a broad knowledge of the literature, Scudder brought to her courses a personal conviction and experience that gave special urgency to her message. Her goal as a teacher was to inspire life rather than to instill convictions; yet to give an impartial treatment or analysis of a literary work was never her style. She resolved this dilemma by candidly admitting her own biases, which the student could, then or later, discount. This practice she adhered to in both her writing and her teaching. In her own college days she had witnessed the struggles of so many friends against the narrowness of religious formulae. Her mother's influence, guided as she was by the teachings of Frederick Denison Maurice and Phillips Brooks, coupled with the experience in Europe surrounded by sacred art and beautiful liturgy, had given Vida Scudder a faith integrated and alive which preserved her. But the realities of her adult life often led Scudder to question not faith but loyalty to institutional religion.

## The Life of the Spirit in the Modern English Poets

In that same year, 1895, Scudder's first major work of literary criticism was published, *The Life of the Spirit in the Modern English Poets*. Her master's thesis for Smith College, published in two parts in the *Andover Review* (1887), was the basis of the first section of the book, "Science and the Modern Poets," in which she discussed "the power of the imagination to assimilate the elements which form the scientific spirit." According to Scudder, science, democracy, and reverence for the past were the forces exerting the strongest influence on the poetry of the nineteenth century. Beginning with Wordsworth and concluding with Tennyson and Browning, Scudder considered the impact of these forces on the spiritual ideals of the major poets rather than on their artistic form. In a sense she carefully limited the scope of her study, deliberately passing over the poets who did not manifest this influence. Despite this caveat, however, one of the major criticisms of this book was her exclusion of works that disputed or did not fit into her prearranged thesis.[3]

Science did not destroy art because it dispelled mystery but rather, by extending knowledge, science gave the poet a broader perception of vaster regions still unknown. In contrast with earlier poetry, Scudder showed that the nature poems of the modern age had a far greater delicacy thanks to discoveries of the natural sciences. She pointed out many instances in the poetry of Shelley, Wordsworth, Tennyson, and Browning where the poets anticipated evolutionary developments. Progress, growth, development, whether in nature, character, or thought processes, had added new dimensions to the poetry of the age, and were a direct result of evolutionary thought so vital in the nineteenth century. At this time Scudder was influenced by Fabian socialism and its gradualist approach. In contrast to the popular Social Darwinism which posited a static society controlled by the fittest, Scudder saw a continuous social evolution as the basis for her optimistic socialist theories. However, even when she moved beyond Fabianism she continued to speak of the need for a gradually evolving socialist character. More important still, science had revealed a unifying force connecting all things in nature, a force which the poetic imagination had often seen before. Science had not yet discovered what this omnipresent force was, but the poets, said Scudder, boldly proclaimed it God (55).

Still science was not an unmixed blessing. That unity it revealed might become a leveler; an awareness of the forces in nature might result in fatalism; a preoccupation with facts and minutiae could fetter the imagination. To Scudder the best safeguard against such dangers was the nature of poetry and the poet because the function of the imagination was to interpret the world of wonder that science revealed (51–55).

By the end of the century Scudder's earlier interest in the natural sciences had shifted to the social sciences. The scientific revolution seemed a thing of the past, whereas the democratic revolution, she felt, had only just begun. Despite the advances made in the nineteenth century, the real work in establishing a true democracy was ahead. The evolutionary process revealed in nature applied to advances in political and social maturation as well. Thus she saw a similar democratic force exerting a powerful influence on the poetic mind. Scudder saw Wordsworth as the chief exemplar of the democratic spirit. Certainly Shelley gave greater impulse to the revolutionary movement in the early years of the century, but Wordsworth's poetry in all its varieties showed the permanence of the ideal of the revolution. Instead of the revolutionary-turned-Tory, Scudder saw in Wordsworth's later work a loyalty to his central convictions: the worth of the plain people, simplicity of life, and the dignity of labor. Because he recognized that democracy, to survive at all, must move beyond the mere political to the economic and industrial, she hailed Wordsworth as the pioneer of modern social thought (69–93).

The third force at work in modern poetry was a reverence for the past. Three periods—the Hellenic, Medieval, and Renaissance—had a special force or drawing power for modern poets, but their quest for a home in the past was only a temporary refuge from a sordid present. The same spiritual restlessness drove them just as surely back to the present (145–200).

Although nineteenth-century poetry was not dominated by a Dante or a Shakespeare, it was nevertheless expressive of the age. The hope of the Romantic revolutionaries gave way to the doubt of the Victorians but led to a clearer vision in the faith of

Robert Browning (297–333). Browning had been the subject of several of Scudder's earlier essays, one of these selected by the Boston Browning Society to be included in a representative collection of the work of that society in the past decade.[4] Her chapter, "Browning as a Humorist," shows her real power in literary criticism. She saw Browning as subtle, sophisticated, realistic, and obscure only for those who lacked faith or a sense of humor. Here she analyzed his method as well as his spirit. Browning's mocking at the absurdity of life was, on closer look, his earnest appreciation of the sacredness of life. To Scudder his humor did not end in scoffing but in genuine faith (201–38).

Although *The Life of the Spirit* was conceived as a whole, each chapter in the book could stand as a separate essay linked to the whole by the spiritual ideal revealed. The chapter, "Ideals of Redemption, Medieval and Modern," for example, is a careful analytical discussion and comparison of *The Divine Comedy, The Faerie Queen,* and *Prometheus Unbound,* and shows her intellectual power in exploring the field of ideas. This and the chapter, "Browning as a Humorist," are the best examples of her ability as critic, no doubt because these topics are more carefully defined than some of the others. Scudder wrote fluently, eloquently, but often too diffusely. In her surveys every spiritual impulse seemed to be a movement toward Christianity, just as every humane tendency or stirring of social awareness led her directly to socialism. Her definitions of Christianity or socialism are not yet clear. What is clear is Scudder's growing preoccupation with social issues and with Christian Socialist thought. Often this thought is too obviously or too hurriedly applied to literature. *The Life of the Spirit* must have been in progress during a leave of absence from Wellesley College from 1893 to 1895. The first year she spent working with Helena Dudley in the opening of Denison House in Boston's South End and the second in studying at the Sorbonne. She and Helena Dudley had been actively involved in unionizing the largely Irish-immigrant women workers in the settlement neighborhood.[5] This may account for the obvious intrusions of her own socialist interpretations and her longing for the poet of the new age who would "sing the cause of labor, the unity of the race, the high society to be" (94).

## Social Ideals in English Letters

During these same years Scudder planned the course for which she was most famous at Wellesley, "Social Ideals in English Letters." In her autobiography *On Journey* she spoke of this course as "the most original and significant contribution" that she had to make to the teaching of English literature and as the "permanent link" between her "love of letters" and her "social concern." Because of her active involvement in the settlements and in the labor movement and because her socialist views were well known, the course met with "administrative disapproval and departmental indifference." For the same reasons student response was enthusiastic. Such a course demanded constant vigilance against a "personal slant of opinion," and Scudder realized she was skating "on the thinnest of ice" but she was confident that "the ice never broke." Because she believed that the teacher should be but "the pane of glass" through which the students saw all life, she was careful to present conservative as well as radical and liberal viewpoints (pp. 127–31). A reading list for the course, published in the *Wellesley Alumnae Magazine* in 1926–1927, called for critical readings in the general background of each period as well as in-depth readings from representative authors, radical, liberal, or conservative.

The book, *Social Ideals in English Letters,* made no claim to be all-inclusive. Here she looked at literature as a series of social documents, not simply because great literature revealed the social life of the time nor because of the influence society had on art forms, but because she saw hidden in the literature a vision, a yearning, a forecast of social tendencies or directions. Proceeding chronologically, Scudder showed these social documents moving from the individual to the collective. First came the individual struggle; then as the race grew older, the individual became a type of character, and then, of class or of social group. Such an approach, she knew, meant passing over some of the recognized literary masters, over whole periods and art forms. While this selectivity again led to much criticism, Scudder's distinctive approach to literature required the difficult and subtle skills of dealing with ideals and spiritual impulses.[6]

*Social Ideals* is a veritable pilgrimage through English literature. Her survey began in the seventh century as England came in contact with Christianity. Scudder saw an amazing spiritual change accompanied by a social change just as revolutionary. The annals of monasticism revealed simply the hero-warrior forsaking the world and becoming a peaceful agricultural worker. But the transformation went much deeper, and Scudder showed in the once-proud warrior a new tenderness and a new consciousness of the poor as well as a sense of fellowship with all living things. For Christianity, even though surrounded by barbarism, moved steadily "toward social equality, toward simplification of desires, toward common, active, loving fellowship in the productive arts of peace" (13). Fellowship, simplicity, peace were ideals increasingly important to Scudder in later years. Fellowship was an almost mystical experience, a sustaining force in her work for social equality. Simplicity of life she urged on the many religious and social groups she worked with; still, arriving at a simple life was a lifelong personal struggle. Peace was essential to a just society, although pacifism was a position she reached only after great soul-searching.[7]

By the tenth century the monasteries had fallen from their high ideals, and by the fourteenth even the mendicants had become an "unmitigated nuisance." Nevertheless, even at their worst the monks and friars preserved the example of a "common life for common ends" and at their best handed on the "tradition of a pure Christian communism vowed to democratic fellowship and to personal poverty" (10–16).

By the later Middle Ages the social structure of society had become fixed; no age produced a more aristocratic literature than the Middle Ages. Though Chaucer had made the common folk live, they were shown as occupying an inferior status, and, said Scudder, would not have resented their creator's condescension. All this was part of a feudal system "sure of its own finality and little likely to foster social discontent" (16–17). Periodically renewed religious impulses had tried to restore the spirit of unworldliness of the ancient monasteries, but the basic structure of the society remained untouched. The marked contrasts in medieval life were obvious to the intellectuals and the students, and the goliardic poetry and animal epics reveal the oppression of the poor at the hands of both the Church and the nobles.

But a new class-consciousness and indignation was stirring among the English working class, and William Langland voiced the bitter cry of the people in words and tone the people could understand. The peasant revolts and uprisings that followed failed, and Langland and his poem were forgotten. The poem failed as art, too, yet *Piers Plowman* was prophetic of a distinct industrial movement and, to Scudder, struck a modern note in the religious significance it accorded to labor. No previous work in an age of feudalism had presented so subversive an idea as this in which the worker was seen as the center of the social order. Langland had found the heart of socialism although the basic framework of society in his poem remained untouched. Scudder hailed him as "perhaps the first Englishman thoughtfully to dwell on the social power of the faith of Christ" (24–45). But the prayerful, almost contemplative mood she created with Langland's challenge to Christians is jarred by her own answer to his appeal, "a voluntary Christian Socialism in the midst of a rigid social order and an unheeding world" (45).

In the next few centuries the voice of the laborer was lost in the burst of intellectual energy in the Renaissance. Here the cultured statesman of the period, Thomas More, spoke for the poor with ideas so daring that his *Utopia* became a popular term. Even the most revolutionary of social critics, Scudder felt, would agree with More's central thought that as long as there was property and while money was the standard of all other things a nation could neither be governed justly nor happily (56). She considered Thomas More superior to the most modern utopian writers. The redistribution of labor was no new idea to utopians or socialists, but More made labor universal and compulsory rather than voluntary. In More she found the seeds of many social theories and movements of later ages. For example, his plan for a six-hour working day was possible even in a pre-industrial society with the suppression of luxuries and the elimination of the leisure class. Particularly striking was More's call for greater simplicity of life, and this as England entered her golden age (63–66).

The approach of these two major social prophets, Langland accepting the rigidity of society but calling for social regeneration and More hoping with the ardor of a revolutionary for social reconstruction, were to Vida Scudder the two basic paths of modern social radicals. However, More spoke with greater force because his faith in the Christian message demanded that he seek a new social order, not simply personal regeneration as did Langland (77).

Scudder found little trace of unrest in the literature of the next few centuries. Men and women concentrated on building a national character, and this evolution was important in the advance of democracy. In the seventeenth century leaders were obsessed by religious matters and were little concerned with the actual conditions in which people lived. The Restoration momentarily diverted this concentration, and though the reaction to the frivolity of the Restoration came quickly, Vida Scudder deplored the fact that in moving away from the ignoble, leaders sought the respectable rather than the ideal (80–89).

Despite surface similarities, the eighteenth century, Vida Scudder believed, had less in common with those entering the twentieth century than had the earlier ages. The literature had become the literature of the sophisticated. The social satire was keen and clever but its range was limited. However, this century did succeed in separating religion and politics from social concerns. Politics had often ignored social needs, but the indifference of the church in this age had parallel for Scudder only in the present day. Successful in its long struggle against Romanism and Puritanism, the Anglican Church had lost sight of its ideal. The followers of Christ had become now in theory, as so often in practice, champions of "established rights and of the well-to-do" rather than the champions of "liberty and the poor." To Vida Scudder the tragedy of this age was best exemplified in the career and writings of Jonathan Swift. Though Swift bitterly denounced the society and politics of his age, he made no appeal to men to fight against the evils he described. The entirely orthodox Dean Swift had no conception at all "of power for salvation, either individual or social, inherent in the Gospel of Christ" (90–112).

The literature of the nineteenth century was distinctly different. Ushered in by the French Revolution, the scene had been set by an upheaval quieter but of far greater depth and requiring drastic readjustments in the entire social system. This Industrial Revolution had been working powerfully below the surface, "reaching chiefly the inarticulate." Now it had moved to the forefront, demanding the attention of all groups and classes of society. Recalling the attitude of both politics and religion to society in the eighteenth century, Scudder was not surprised that in this time of tremendous social change both were found wanting (115–17).

To Scudder, not even the poets, the great literary heirs of the Revolution, were aware of the force of industrialism at work in society. She acknowledged their valiant attempt to effect social change by their work but offered no further analysis of their poetry. Whether Scudder considered the power of these poets too great for a general overview, or whether she felt she had considered the poets in her previous book, *The Life of the Spirit,* her decision to dismiss them so summarily does destroy the balance of this survey (117–19). She was evidently more concerned with developing the thought of her literary guides to socialism. The rest of the book, almost two thirds of the study, is given over to discussion of the Victorian prose writers and the steady trend of thought toward social justice.

Scudder turned first to the fiction of the mid-nineteenth century with its quickening interest in social types and its awareness of social unrest. Dickens and Thackeray presented a cleavage of classes not seen before in English literature, but they did not delve beneath the surface of society or question the deeper forces at work. Yet, to Scudder, the unjust social system that prevailed was a glaring fact. The world of Dickens with its preoccupation with the material existed in order that the world of Thackeray might be freed from such sordid care. Both societies were commercial to the core, but if the novelists were aware of the crudeness of the societies they depicted, they were not able to explain it (134–42).

Fortunately, George Eliot carried the social survey of Dickens and Thackeray a step further. Eliot's best works, *Silas Marner, Adam Bede, Mill on the Floss,* dealt with the England of her childhood, not invaded by the spiritual unrest of the industrial age. As Eliot turned from the past to the England around her she saw the seething forces of unrest. Eliot wrote not of a class but of a sympathy in the heart of a small group for those who were hard-pressed by society. Most of the characters in such works as *Romola, Middlemarch,* and *Daniel Deronda* have redeeming traits and personal integrity. But alongside these are new figures, such as Dorothea or Lydgate, not quite sure of their way but seeking somehow to be one with the suffering humanity around them. In Dorothea, Scudder saw a transitional figure, going beyond the soft-hearted ladies of Thackeray and Dickens, but not yet prepared to take her part with the forces working for righteousness. The social conscience was at last alive (180–93). This social unrest was even more forcefully expressed in the ethical novels such as Charles Kingsley's *Alton Locke.* Kingsley's solution for the problem was Christianity, a solution Scudder found somewhat apocalyptic since he offered to the Church no real answers to the problems as she saw them. Like the criticism that would be made of her own work, Scudder found the reformer and the artist  coexisting so strongly in Kingsley that neither was able to develop its full potential (197).

Thomas Carlyle, John Ruskin, and Matthew Arnold dominated the literary scene at mid-century, and a major portion of Scudder's book is devoted to the social criticism of these writers. While they testified to the truth of the social scenes depicted by Dickens and Thackeray, they also analyzed, sought causes, and presented proposals for restructuring society.

Thomas Carlyle's *Sartor Resartus* was a forerunner of the scientific and social analysis of society of modern times. Scudder pointed out that his underlying thesis dismissed the idea of society as a social contract and stressed rather the unity, the fellowship required. And in Carlyle's reverence for the laborers who toiled that he might live she found at last an echo of the thought of Langland. Yet Carlyle was no readier than Langland to urge the laborers to initiate reform (151–56, 214–16).

John Ruskin's social criticism was a direct outcome of his efforts to foster in England an aesthetic revival. The root cause of the ugliness in English cities Ruskin traced to the conditions imposed on the workers by the modern industrial system. Even more dangerous in his eyes was the complacency with which society accepted these conditions. Ruskin believed that all art must be the expression of a common life, but the mechanical character of modern industry had destroyed spontaneity, all impulse toward creativity, in the working class. Scudder called on her experience in the settlements and at Wellesley to illustrate. The professional classes worked just as hard as manual laborers, but their work was life, for it employed and cultivated the higher faculties and, however strenuous, was interesting. The work in factory or stockyard, in contrast, had been so dehumanized that the workers' real life must be outside their trade. For this reason, insisted Scudder, the laborers must have shorter working days and leisure for cultural pursuits (166–67). This was only one aspect of Ruskin's call for a moralizing of industry that would bring freedom to the nation as a whole. More humane factory methods, shorter hours, permanent contracts, a just wage, and a just price were other parts of his scheme for renewing the industrial relations of society. Most important, in Vida Scudder's view, was his call for a new social ethic as he nagged at the apathetic to evolve a new morality in tune with the new mercantile and industrial age. Scudder found few passages in Ruskin more challenging, more pertinent to the modern industrial scene, than his chapter, "The Roots of Honor," in *Unto This Last* asking why society did not demand the same service and sacrifice from the merchants and employers as it expected of its doctors, clergymen, or soldiers in time of crisis (222). In the next few years Scudder made a similar point in her own writings dealing directly with socialism.

Even in Ruskin's earlier works Scudder had discovered a profound longing for simplicity, a virtue difficult to achieve in an industrial society. But from Tolstoy in Russia to Thoreau and Whitman in America it was a constant theme, and Scudder insisted that there was a special message here for the new century (227–29).

The third writer of this group, Matthew Arnold, was more lacking in democratic instincts than either Ruskin or Carlyle, yet more convinced that democracy alone could remedy the evils he saw in society. Arnold spoke not of mere political democracy but of social democracy, the establishing of a social equality which would lead to real change in social conditions. When he realized that he spoke in vain to the middle class, Arnold turned to the workers and urged them to take the initiative, not just in their own behalf but for the national good as well. Here for the first time in English literature Scudder found a writer urging a worker to assume the initiative for social salvation. To Scudder, Arnold's proposals were more practical than those of Carlyle or Ruskin: a redistribution of wealth, especially wealth based on property, a genuine municipal system, and public schools for the middle class. Yet Scudder criticized Arnold because he took issue with socialist thought and feared the danger of too "rapid progress of an uninformed democracy" (271–73). Such hesitancy she felt was for a former age; modern critics were moved to action.

Scudder summed up Victorian literature as the "literature of the Privileged hailing the Unprivileged as masters of the future." Succeeding generations would find in this literature the same stirring of social conscience, the same search for a synthesis of democracy and authority that she found in the literature of the past. That synthesis she felt would be the socialist state (275).

In her concluding chapter, "Contemporary England," Scudder abandoned any attempt at literary analysis. Modern visionaries, stirred by that same social passion she found in literature of past ages, moved from art to action, from thought to deed. The best example of this shifting emphasis was the "Fabian Essays"—good literature, but the authors "wavering between literature and life" (287). Because of this same wavering, *Social Ideals in English Literature* falls short of great literary criticism. But it is important for any understanding of the life and work of Vida Scudder. Hers was a lifetime of study and meditating on the classics of Western civilization, and the book remains the great tribute to her love of letters and her social concern. Her penetrating study of Langland, More, and Swift is literary criticism at its best, and her rhythmic prose and careful diction carry the reader along the paths she treads with little hesitation. Scudder's strength is seen in the medieval section of the book although it would be years later before she realized that her real literary home was in this period. The detours here, as she stopped to interject short notes on socialism, are momentary distractions. However, as she moved into the contemporary period, the bulk of the work, she strayed more often from literary criticism, and the exposition frequently becomes a polemic. Her style also suffers. The smooth compelling prose of the first is often monotonous and repetitious in the later chapters. Scudder tended to write on a large plan, to generalize. Readers of all persuasions could sympathize with Langland's or More's searching observations. Had she written more precisely here, her interpretations would have met sharper criticism but might have generated more critical discussion of the role of the church or the worker in modern society, or even of socialist theory. Caught up in the modern struggle, Scudder, like many of her Fabians, abandoned literature for life. For Scudder this was a deliberate choice in 1897, in order to "help a little to make ready the way for the workers who may come in the fairer civilization we long for . . ."[8]

## The "Tainted Money" Controversy

Scudder's commitment to use her talents to build a fairer civilization met an unexpected test within the college in the next year. Unlike so many of the radical reformers of her day Scudder never discounted the value of her middle-class education. She may even have mentally exalted the role of the college in society in order to justify remaining at a post so congenial in every way to her temperament yet so at odds with the life she saw in the settlement neighborhoods. At this time young Wellesley, like so many other colleges, was intent on raising money for buildings and endowments. A proposed gift from Rockefeller moved the faculty to question the propriety of accepting such gifts. Initially, Scudder organized these faculty and student protests. But she was in a dilemma, for she realized the repercussions her actions might have on the college. She sought the advice of her uncle, Horace Scudder, himself a trustee. In a long letter to his niece Horace Scudder urged her to be more conciliatory. Her individual letters to board members reflect this advice. She expressed very clearly her personal concern and urged them to consider carefully the public distrust that surrounded such money.[9] She also paid a visit to the author of *Wealth Against Commonwealth* (1894), the first documented exposé of the trusts and of Standard Oil in particular, Henry D. Lloyd, who was then living in Boston. She was surprised when he explained that denunciation was a disagreeable duty which must be done at times "but the really interesting work was the study of constructive forces and experiments."[10] Such advice suited Scudder's temperament better than protest, and, in conjunction with Bishop H. C. Potter of Central New York and the Reverend Charles Brent, rector of Saint Stephen's Church in Boston, she organized a conference to be held late in June at Saint Stephen's to discuss "the question of the right relation of Churches, Charities and Institutions of Learning to money won by methods which the moral sense of the community is beginning to distrust:"[11]

By this time the gift to Wellesley was secure, but several of the trustees attended the meeting. The detailed minutes of the meeting in the Brent Papers reveal the confusion of mind among the more socially concerned people in the country. The following November (1900) her article "Ill Gotten Gifts to Colleges" prepared originally for the college newspaper, appeared in the *Atlantic Monthly*. Here she reiterated her belief that one of the most pressing duties of the academic and religious world was to strengthen the growing demand in the country "that the method of acquiring wealth come wholly under the dominion of the moral sense."[12]

Underlying all this was the larger question of personal loyalty that Scudder had to resolve for herself. She seriously considered resigning from Wellesley, but most of her colleagues told her that the "deeper loyalty" demanded that she stay on at the college. Henry D. Lloyd wrote to her that it was "certainly worth a great deal more to us to have you inside Wellesley now than it ever has been, and you can do more good there in this matter inside than you could possibly do outside." She remained at Wellesley, but the physical and mental strain of living her life on so many levels was becoming more evident. Horace Scudder had noted in his diary that she was in "a strained and somewhat unnatural state," and in February of the following year her health broke down completely. The doctor's prescription that she give herself over to something entirely different for the next two years was not an unwelcome remedy.[13]

## Chapter Three

# Italian Days and New Directions

### A Listener in Babel

In May, 1901, Vida Scudder was well enough to go abroad accompanied by her mother and Florence Converse, now a colleague in the work at Denison House. After months of idle wandering through the English countryside she spent the next year on the Continent, wrote sonnets and verses, and was at length able to put the events of the past decade in perspective. Physically well enough now to use her leisure in writing, she worked on a novel, a "queer (modern) Franciscan sort of book—called *A Listener in Babel*," she wrote to Jane Addams, which "has been on hand a long while."[1] The book was one of the many radical or socialist novels that appeared at the beginning of the century, and Vida Scudder was more intent on the ideas than on plot or character.

*A Listener in Babel* is a thinly veiled autobiographical account of Scudder's own experiences during the past decade and of her gradual conversion to socialism.[2] The heroine Hilda, a talented young artist, after a happy but abnormal childhood of sheltered privilege travelling with her mother, hoped to cure the sense of unreality that had plagued her life by spending a year in one of the college settlements. The conversations with her mother and later with the members of the academic community at her alma mater revealed all the arguments against the settlement movement. At Langley House Hilda assumed the role of listener, for the residents represented every possible view, from the sedate charity-worker, Miss Harding, to the fiery anarchist, Janet Frothingham.

Added to these were the direct contacts with the people of the neighborhood, either in the artificial atmosphere of the House or in their ordinary setting. Hilda's confusion continued as she took part in meetings held at Langley House to discuss trade-unions versus socialism, economic distress in the neighborhood, and the moral obligation of the colleges toward doubtful benefactions. After a visit to the pastor of an uptown parish Hilda might have despaired had she not been rescued by a fellow resident and taken off to a retreat. Here Father Phillips, the labor priest, restored her faith in a church invisible and introduced her to the prophets of freedom, Isaiah, Saint Francis, Saint Thomas More. After two years in the settlement Hilda decided on her future. Helped by two of the women from the neighborhood, she planned to go into the factories to learn the trades and to study the possible field for handicrafts in modern industry.

*A Listener in Babel* was submitted to the publishers early in 1901, before its author's breakdown. In a long letter to his niece, then recuperating in Italy, Horace Scudder spoke frankly about the book. She had been physically unwell while writing it, and he suggested that she set it aside and revise it when she was feeling better.[3] No doubt Vida took his advice, but the book published two years later had many of the same failings he described in his lengthy letter.

*A Listener in Babel* attracted little attention from the critics. Perhaps the path Hilda took sounded more utopian than socialist to the general reader. Scudder's purpose was to concentrate on "man thinking," not as a philosophical study of ideas, but as a revelation of thought at its most vivid, as "irradiate with personality it flashes from mind to mind" (Foreword, viii). This was the interplay Scudder enjoyed most in the academic world and in the life of the settlement. Denison House had become a center for liberal and radical thinkers of all classes and persuasions, and Vida Scudder relished these contacts. However, the animated discussions in which she had been involved over the past decade are not translated to the written page.

The dialogue starts off clear, direct, but too often becomes a lengthy exposition of an idea. The conversations are a series of separate episodes or chapters and, except for their impact on Hilda, do not become an integral part of the progress of the novel. For this reason the characters, carefully drawn at the outset, do not develop. Young Hilda is able to make many of the choices the author could not or would not make. But even Hilda is described, rather than revealed through the dialogues, as "one of those rare persons to whom deepest reality can only come through fellowship with the general experience, whether of joy or pain" (4). To Scudder such natures as Hilda's, Janet Frothingham's, or Lawrence Ferguson's appearing in private life were a sign of the spiritual democracy for which she longed. In contrast, the characters from Hilda's past life, her mother, her cousin Howard Brown, Mr. Wilkinson the wealthy minister, while not exactly caricatures, have few, if any, redeeming features. The contrast between the home of Hilda's wealthy cousin, Howard Brown, and the college settlement on Lincoln Street is sharply drawn in the novel and her cousin's reaction to a service in Saint George's in the city was typical of the aristocratic idea of Christianity the author found so distressing.[4] In the novel when the heroine Hilda enters the vestry of the First Church on fashionable Webster Avenue, she is surprised and troubled by her conversation with the pastor. Afterwards, crushed in spirit, she drops into a church where Evensong is being sung by a small group of women, and an "empty-faced young priest" knocked "great words about sin and atonement against each other till they sounded hollow" (156). What Uncle Horace Scudder had written of the first draft is true of the book: ". . . it ignores almost wholly the honest life of those who fail to take just the attitude of your heroine and her associates."[5]

For all its faults, *A Listener in Babel* is important for what it reveals of Vida Scudder as the emerging social critic. How Hilda adjusted her relations, social and spiritual, to the economic realities was indeed a significant part of Scudder's life story. Almost all the situations or conversations in *A Listener in Babel* are based on incidents in Vida Scudder's life. In fact, Chapter X, "Learning and Mammon," is almost a verbatim account of the meeting held at

Saint Stephen's Church, Boston, in 1900 to discuss the question of "tainted money."[6] In the book, Henrietta Morse, a young economics teacher at Huntington University, voiced Vida Scudder's view at the time while Hilda, the silent listener, reflected the author's mental anguish as she heard other convincing arguments. Henrietta, too, struggled with the question of loyalty and was advised that resigning from the college was "to abandon the rising generation" (209).

Many of the ideas expressed here had already been presented in Scudder's three earlier works, *The Witness of Denial, The Life of the Spirit in the Modern English Poets,* and *Social Ideals in English Letters.* Others had been tested in socialist and religious journals and were explored further here. *A Listener in Babel* in its genteel fashion was far more visionary than many of the protest novels of the day. Scudder was moving toward a more radical socialism. Hilda, in the novel, had experienced firsthand "the futility of all philanthropic effort in a competitive civilization" and at length agreed that instead of helping the poor to cope with their situations the residents should be teaching them to rebel (125, 136). Although Hilda had not the explosive temperament of her anarchist friend, she did catch from her a glimpse of an America that would someday learn to utilize the best gifts of the immigrants, a vision of an America transcending boundaries of race and creed.

This need for a moral unity in the country was to become an essential part of Scudder's socialist thought (79–82). Though she had long called herself a socialist, she was still wrestling with certain tenets of political socialism that did not harmonize with her Christian principles. To bridge the gap that existed between the classes, to learn from the poor as well as to work for them, these had been her motives in going to the settlement. She had met labor leaders in free discussions in the Brotherhood of the Carpenter, at Denison House, and in the Church Socialist League. At Denison House she had been instrumental in organizing the women workers in the neighborhood and had even been elected as one of the representatives to the Central Labor Union. But few of the settlement workers or labor leaders accepted even her earlier moderate socialist views. In *A Listener in Babel* the class antagonism of O'Hagan, the labor leader, grieved Hilda, but she recognized that his hostility was no greater than that of many of the rich that she knew. In fact, the loyalty to an abstract idea that she had seen among workers of such different backgrounds, races, and religions impressed her, while the class struggle and the violence upon which it depended troubled her. "There will be a holier expression of brotherhood some day than any based, like that, on the class-fight theory," mused Hilda after a long talk with O'Hagan. To work this out was Scudder's major challenge in the next few years (182).

Yet, on the whole, the radical leaders in *A Listener in Babel* fared much better than did the Protestantism that Scudder felt had failed in its obligation toward the immigrants and the workers and thus toward society as a whole. Scudder sounds startlingly relevant here as she criticized the institutional church, yet remained loyal to it as the guardian of the only ideal that could save. This was due in large part to the influence of the Italian saints at a critical period in her own life.

### Saint Catherine of Siena

In 1901 Vida Scudder could not have found a place better suited to her present physical needs and to her intellectual and spiritual delight than Italy. The history and art of the Middle Ages surrounded her and brought back memories of months in Europe in her childhood. While poking around antique stalls and bookstores she came across the biography of Saint Catherine by Fra Raimondo of Capua, her confessor, and copies of her letters. The letters were the spiritual ballast Vida Scudder's soul needed as Catherine revealed her own interior struggles and the turmoil of mind of some of the closest of her "famiglia." For months Catherine was her constant companion, and ideas for a historical romance were taking shape. When the publisher J. M. Dent suggested that she prepare an English edition of the letters of Saint Catherine, Vida Scudder accepted the challenge.

Back in Boston, she was tutored in the finer points of the Italian language and steeped herself in the history of the Italian saints and the medieval church. Saint Catherine, she discovered, was not a Dante or a Petrarch, could scarcely write. The letters, dictated to willing secretaries, were often hurried, intense, enthusiastic, and always more intent on the message than the style. Yet Catherine was able to accomplish what neither gifted poets, nor political leaders, nor powerful prelates could; she persuaded Pope Gregory XI to return to Rome thus ending the seventy year sojourn of the Popes at Avignon. But if Scudder found Catherine careless of style, she considered her "psychologically astute" in identifying with the person she addressed. To Pope Gregory XI, she offered continual challenge; to Pope Urban, she counselled moderation; to fellow religious, she advised watchfulness over movements of the heart and ever greater desire; and to her confessor, Raimondo, she revealed in utter simplicity the struggles and the mystical graces at work in her soul.[7]

The great variety of people with whom Catherine came in contact revealed different facets of the saint's own personality. Vida Scudder's careful selection of and her brief introduction to each letter made this edition a short biography as well, so clearly does the character of Catherine emerge from the letters. Scudder was always the teacher, and the letters selected pictured the society of that day, too, for her heroine could only be understood against this background. Scudder did not presume on the reader's knowledge of medieval or church history but prepared a brief outline of the political events of Catherine's time and another of the highlights of the saint's life (18–22). Where possible, Scudder tried to group the letters and to be selective within the group. "Letters on the Consecrated Life," for example, contain Catherine's counsels to a hermit, to a Dominican nun, and to the wife of a tailor. Many of the letters discuss the interior struggles of Catherine's individual disciples, and her advice often struck a responsive chord in Vida Scudder. So in the introduction as well as in the letters themselves, ideas that were to be themes in Scudder's later writings emerge, as well as thoughts that were to buoy her up in her own struggles. Catherine's successes were too often a dismal failure in that the external achievement did not accomplish the spiritual goal she had in mind. Gregory XI's return to Rome did not heal the division in the Church; on the contrary, his successor Urban's attempts at reform led to the Great Schism even in Catherine's lifetime. Catherine felt such disappointments keenly, hence her oft-quoted advice, "Care not to present a finished work to God Who is Infinite Love and demands from thee only infinite desire," came from the heart of one who had experienced both success and failure, and the failure of success (ii, 70). Yet Catherine never counselled her followers to retreat from the world but only to increase their desire for the Good. Catherine's belief that the Church was an image of that pure universal fellowship that must exist if people were to live in peace spoke directly to Scudder, who at that time saw lack of spiritual unity as the greatest weakness in American democracy.

This detailed study of the life and letters of Saint Catherine had its greatest impact on Vida Scudder herself and cleared the way, mentally and spiritually, for the role she was to play in the church and in society. Catherine had revealed to her the importance of loyalty to one's vision of the truth. Loyalty was a natural virtue for Vida Scudder, but already in her short career conflicting loyalties had caused great inner turmoil and grief. Her own religious upbringing had enabled her to distinguish between loyalty to the faith of Christ and to the institutional church. But her intimacy with the saint carried her further and made her bolder in her loyalty to Christ and His church. The church was a living body constantly growing, changing, adapting itself to the needs of the time, as it continued Christ's redemptive mission. Therefore, as an educator, Scudder determined to make the church in America aware of the pressing problems stemming from industrialization. She became increasingly active in radical Christian Socialist groups both within and without the church and was the leading spokeswoman for this view in the Episcopal Church in the early twentieth century.

### The Disciple of a Saint

Vida Scudder saw Saint Catherine as the "prototype of all modern women idealists."[8] Catherine had prepared herself spiritually before she emerged into public life and devoted herself to the obvious needs of the poor and the sick in Siena. Gradually she became involved in the political feuds in her native town and in the neighboring cities of Italy. Out of necessity she moved to a wider stage, for she had seen beyond the dissension in the Church, the worldliness of its prelates, and the indifference of its Popes to a Church that must be a House of Reconciliation if people were to live in peace and unity. Loyal to this vision of the truth in spite of numerous obstacles, Catherine gathered around her disciples who would help in the work and be helped by it. Vida Scudder had felt herself one of these disciples as she worked on the *Letters of St. Catherine*; her novel, *The Disciple of a Saint,* almost wrote itself.[9]

Raniero di Landoccio dei Pagliaresi (Neri) was a highly educated young man of Siena, cultured, poetic, sensitive, and somewhat melancholic. Soured by the scandals in the Church and by the lives of the clergy in the small towns, Neri still had a yearning for perfection. Neri first saw Catherine as she was ministering to the plague-stricken outside Siena. Her charity, energy, and strength of purpose attracted him, and he became one of the most devoted and best loved of her *famiglia.* Neri became Catherine's secretary, and this imaginary biography of Neri, based on facts gleaned from the letters, is largely the story of Catherine's influence on him. Neri had the natural talents of a diplomat save for his brooding Hamlet-like hesitancy, especially in things spiritual or political. Sent as Catherine's messenger to Gregory XI at Avignon, Neri came under the influence of the pagan revival and enjoyed the intellectual stimulus of his new friends. One of these told him of the Pope's secret vow that if elected, he would restore the papal seat to Rome. Neri hesitated to use this information and left his audience with the Pope filled with pity for the head of Christendom. While awaiting Catherine's arrival at Avignon, Neri climbed Mont Ventoux. The rationalizing influence of his friends at Avignon won out as he climbed, and Neri no longer felt moral despair at the failure of the Church. Rather than expect a Church made of men to translate the Divine into the common life, each must press on in his own way to union with the Divine. But on this mountaintop, as a hermit or as an intellectual, Neri's peace was short-lived. Whenever he sought solitude, a deeper quest for unity returned to trouble him. Like Catherine identifying herself with her sinful brothers and sisters, Neri realized that he could not go his own way but must somehow help others to share the vision which was not just for the elect but for all.

Catherine arrived at Avignon and, using the information which Neri himself had hesitated to use, she prevailed upon the Pontiff to return to Rome. Neri's doubts and perplexities prevented him from entering into the work of Catherine at Avignon. Yet fidelity to Catherine kept him on the fringes of her *famiglia* rather than with his learned friends at Avignon, and he followed her to Rome. En route Neri became seriously ill and was cured by Catherine. Yet the old question still tormented him: "Was a visible expression of the Divine idea in the collective life ever possible?" (239).

As Neri had foreseen, the return of Gregory brought neither peace nor unity. Soon after, Gregory died and his successor Urban's attempts at reform led to the Great Schism. To prevent Naples from siding with the anti-pope, Catherine again sent Neri as her delegate, this time much against his will. His cousin Ilaria whom he dearly loved was at the Court of Naples. Here his success with Donna Giovanna was tied to his accepting a dispensation from the anti-pope Clement allowing him to marry his cousin. At first Neri refused, then was about to agree to keep Naples loyal to Rome when news of the death of Catherine reached him. Overcome with remorse that he had even played with the delusion that Catherine or the Church could ever be served by the least departure from strict integrity, he returned to Rome. Kneeling beside the body of Catherine, Neri for the first time knew the secret of the Cross. The problem he had wrestled with since Mont Ventoux was answered. As Scudder explained it: "Where love repentant meets love sacrificial, and meeting, is transformed into its likeness, there is the Church of God! No righteous society, such as he had longed [for] in vain, sought in vain to discover, but humanity in process of redemption" (336).

A historical romance, *The Disciple of a Saint* is a far more carefully constructed novel than Scudder's *A Listener in Babel.* In the latter the characters, though drawn from real life, are more stereotypes than real people. In *The Disciple of a Saint* the plot and major characters are true to the historical record, slim though this may be at times, but the use of the facts and the development of the characters are original. While Catherine is the central figure, Neri remains the hero of this novel as he struggles, through her influence, to remain true to the ideal despite a melancholia which cripples him.

Scudder writes easily and the dialogue on the whole is close to the period. At times her sentences are overlong, often so complicated that the idea is obscured. This is particularly so when she shifts from the novelist to the essayist. For example, Neri is disappointed because his task as Catherine's secretary brought him less peace of mind than did the care of the sick. The reader could understand this problem more readily than Neri's solution:

By degrees he became once more subject to his old painful activity of thought. But he stilled it, to a certain extent, by maintaining the attitude of docile obedience and prayer, and found succour in that constant subjection of personal mood to the expression of a common experience, which is the precious discipline of Catholic worship, helping through the ages to train the race in an emotional unity which serves as corrective to the tyranny of chance desires, and forms the basis of all true harmony in social life (86).

In this involved sentence Scudder was more the lecturer than the teacher, more anxious to tell of the strength of liturgical worship than to allow the reader to discover it through Neri. At other times, too, Scudder is overly anxious to draw the parallels for her readers. When Neri is reluctant to admit to his learned friends at Avignon, even to the Pope, that he was the "spiritual son of an ignorant visionary," the author immediately adds: "The type was familiar at Avignon and was viewed, in the society where he found his natural level, much as 'Salvationists' are viewed on the same level today" (207).

Further on, Scudder interrupted the conversation between Neri and his old friend, Stefano, now Cardinal Frontaigne, to remark somewhat defensively: "Religious melancholia, even more common in those days than in our own, was then generally regarded, per-

haps less superficially than we think, not as delusion but as experience charged with true meaning" (371). Obviously Vida
Scudder's attempts to make the crisis of the fourteenth century
relevant to the twentieth century accounted for such intrusions,
just as her immersion in the letters of Catherine excuse or explain
her sometimes archaic use of the reflexive pronoun. "The part was
taken by a boy who held him haughtily" (18), "Meantime he . . .
held him therefore scrupulously loyal . . ." (265), ". . . And now
he found him strong to contemplate" (337).

Nevertheless, Scudder did get below the surface of medieval
life and treated the political and spiritual issues with sympathy and
honesty: In the twentieth century as in the fourteenth the role of
the Church was often a divisive issue for religious leaders, social
reformers, and searching souls. Like most of the latter, Neri was
bothered more by questions of practice than dogma. For a brief
moment he had caught a glimpse of the Church not as a righteous
society but as "humanity in process of redemption" (336). The
vision left, but this was the faith to which he clung. Catherine, on
the other hand, felt that her sins were the cause of the evils in
the Church. Unlike Neri, Catherine's vision of the Church and its
mission was clear, and she saw in her effort to reform the Church
the desire to aid in the salvation of all. This sense of personal
responsibility for the corporate ills of society was strong in all social
reform movements in the twentieth century. But for Scudder,
Catherine had a special message which refined her own distinction
between loyalty to the faith of Christ and to the institutional
church. She, too, might often grieve over the church's failures,
criticize its lapses but she would be steadied by the saint's vision
of the church—not of a righteous society, but of a society continually
being redeemed. Scudder saw her work in the church as her share
in that process of redemption.

### Democracy in America

At first an answer to a personal and spiritual need, the message
of Saint Catherine guided Scudder in new directions and to a work

in the church that would be the major focus of her energies in the later years of her life. Even while in Italy this influence was apparent as she brooded over her experiences in the previous decade. Once she was able to put these events in proper perspective, Scudder prepared a series of articles on Democracy in America for the *Atlantic Monthly*. In these she confined herself to domestic rather than to foreign affairs which "still kept her awake o'nights." Although she did not dwell on the Spanish-American war in her autobiography, in two long letters at that time to Ann Whitney, a noted Boston sculptor, she spoke frankly of the traumatic effect that the war had on her and on the work she was trying to do. Coming at a time when she was physically and mentally over-wrought, the war and its aftermath had contributed greatly to her illness. But the months in Europe had shown her that America's ills were not so deep-set as those of the Italians or the French. "We have much to expiate," she wrote her friend, "but I believe that God has a great future for us yet."[10] In these articles she looked at the "great experiment" to see wherein it had failed and why, and offered some suggestions.

In the first article of the series, "A Hidden Weakness in Our Democracy," she looked at the many forces that made for disintegration—racial antipathy, religious hostility, and class antagonism—at play in a country dedicated "to the creation of a universal fellowship." This contrast between "our national pretensions and our national achievements" was the basic cause of social discontent (639, 642). The opposition between the privileged and unprivileged, between capital and labor, was only one phase of that disunion. The differences in moral outlook went much deeper and were far more serious. Only by readjusting their intellectual, social, and religious relations with members of these alienated classes could individual Americans hope to further the unity so necessary to a democracy.[11]

In "Democracy and Education" she concluded that the formal education system failed to furnish the unifying force expected of it. The spiritual unity America needed would come not from an increase in knowledge but from an enrichment of life, which really meant an extension of personality. The settlement houses, for all their failings, had been more successful for manual workers than Chautauqua and university extension courses because, by overcoming the gap between the classes, they had been able to find that common ground on which both educated and uneducated could meet.[12] In "Democracy and Society" she went on to show that the common life for which she pleaded did not require new enterprises or new schemes. True democracy was itself a transforming force, and each century produced those agents necessary to advance it to the next stage. In the twentieth century that force must be the professional class. United by their wage-earning status to the manual workers and by mental conditions to the privileged class, the professional classes were the natural links in the formation of that spiritual democracy that Scudder felt must emerge. Before democracy could do its perfect work, men and women must be in democratic relations to one another, not only politically and professionally but socially as well. Settlements had provided one means of approach, but unless such a spirit was carried over into the home, the democracy that America envisioned would remain forever a Utopia.[13]

In "Democracy and the Church" she discussed the alienation of the workers from the church. They were repelled not by defects of dogma or creed but by the failure of the adherents of Christianity to show that their faith was a vital force in their lives whether in the methods used in business, or the standards of luxury by which they lived. Only the practice of a true simplicity of life by those who professed to be Christians and a "social fellowship visibly independent of class divisions" (524–25) would convince the working class that Christianity was a vital force for unity.[14]

## New Directions in Social Action

Vida Scudder returned from Europe early in 1903 filled with new ideas for her teaching and writing. Her ideas always had a strange way of involving her in social action. Within a few months she had organized a small club of better-educated Italians and of interested Americans to help in organizing work among the Italian immigrants in the settlement neighborhood. This Circolo Italo-Americano was operated and financed independently of Denison House, although it met monthly at the settlement. At the same time an Italian department was started at Denison House headed by Scudder. The larger Italian colony was situated some distance from Denison House in Boston's North End. Excellent social work was already being done there. However, Scudder hoped that the cooperation of the residents and the members of the Circolo in working with the poorer immigrants would provide opportunity for Denison House to move beyond mere philanthropy and afford real democratic contacts essential for all sides. For almost a decade Scudder remained the driving force behind both the Circolo Italo-Americano and the Italian department at Denison House, and through her efforts some of the more influential people turned their attention to the Italian question. Those Americans who met the more educated Italians in the Circolo and found friends among them saw the immigrant in a new light and were eager to aid in whatever phase of the work they could.[15] Nevertheless, Scudder has often been criticized by historians for abandoning work among the Italian peasants for the intellectuals.[16] Both she and Helena Dudley admitted that the work among the poorer Italians was done at first, as much if not more, out of gratitude for the gifts brought to America by the better class. Nevertheless they were proud to report to the College Settlements Association that this policy of helping the better-able immigrants to help their own had become, over the years, a hallmark of the work at Denison House. From the outset Scudder had recognized the racial prejudice animating the Immigration Restriction League. The League had its beginnings in 1894, shortly after Denison House opened, and by this time was supported by Boston's leading reformers and settlement workers. Despite the fact that she realized that she was temperamentally unsuited for the daily life of the settlement, Scudder continued to work for the ideal of that larger fellowship to which the settlement was dedicated and to oppose the Anglo-Saxon bias of the Immigration Restriction League.[17]

In *A Listener in Babel* she depicted the various prejudices she had found among the residents working to "uplift" the immigrant when, in fact, America had suppressed the newcomers' best talents by forcing them to "devote all their powers to ministering to our physical wants" (79–82). Where other reformers saw the hopelessness of trying to merge the diverse ethnic groups crowding into America into one distinctive nationality, Vida Scudder dreamed of a mosaic of talents forming the America of the future. From Italy she had written in "Democracy and Education," "For whether we will or no, the Anglo-Saxon is not the American; nor will he, as the centuries advance, remain on our soil in racial isolation . . ." (822). In an address, "The Irish Literary Drama," delivered at the opening of the Twentieth Century Club's series of plays, she brought out a similar point: "The more we uplift and idealize our conception of the diverse elements that are to create America the deeper will be our comprehension of them, and the stronger our power to hold them to their best."[18]

The greater America of which she spoke, though she often couched her ideas in language acceptable to her audience, went beyond the Americanization or assimilation so often connected with settlement work. In "Experiments in Fellowship" she recognized the validity of the criticisms of the immigrants who saw in this process only a vulgarization of their people. Such criticism, she admitted, aroused "a dormant patriotism" in her but strengthened her belief in the great need for a spiritual unity in America. Loyalty could not be taught but could come only from a shared vision of the America to be, where the newcomers felt themselves allies in the struggle for social righteousness.[19]

## Chapter Four

# Christian and Socialist

Vida Scudder had been a member of the Christian Socialist societies in Boston since their inception at the end of the nineteenth century. Most of these were socialist-oriented but espoused no one political philosophy. Through writing, lecturing, and teaching the members hoped to arouse the social conscience of the Christian churches. However, the Christian Socialist movements of the early twentieth century were also politically socialist, and Vida Scudder was now ready to move in this direction. In 1911, after much deliberation and prayer, she joined the Socialist Party. But she was convinced that the official church must also make its voice heard if the workers were to hope for social change along Christian lines. Consequently, she concentrated her efforts in the Church Socialist League, an organization within the Episcopal Church organized in 1911 by Bishop Bernard I. Bell of Grace Church, Chicago, along the lines of a similar group in the Church of England.[1] In extending an invitation to others to join, Vida Scudder, a vice-president of the League, explained that the founders, all card-carrying members of the Socialist Party, were "first and foremost devout Churchmen," who realized that the Church was "larger than 'isms.'" League members recognized that many devout men and women in the church were not of this economic or political view; however, she continued "it is as deadly to suppose that any economic view held by honest minds is inconsistent with loyal Churchmanship as it would be to commit the whole Body with its enduring stress on eternal things to any transitory phase of human theory." The League by its very existence would at least dispel the charge that the church was the "spiritual home of the privileged and reactionary," and, more important, the League hoped to quicken the life

43

of the church by issuing a special call to intercessory prayer over the social wrongs in society. In addition, the League, "with its firm, intelligent and orthodox socialism," hoped for the opportunity to present to men and women in the church, through its organ, *The Social Preparation for the Kingdom of God,* the socialist claims as seen by devout church members rather than as interpreted by enemies of the Creed.[2] Although Scudder felt that the church as such did not and should not espouse any specific political or economic doctrine, the true Christian spirit should move the members as individuals to concern themselves in the vital affairs of the world in which they lived.

She had envisioned for herself a similar educational role in the Society of the Companions of the Holy Cross (S.C.H.C.), where she constantly and successfully urged the members to broaden their perception of social issues. Through the efforts of many such forward-looking groups the Episcopal Church at its General Convention in 1910 appointed a joint Commission of Social Service to study and report upon social conditions, to coordinate the activities of the socially oriented organizations in the church, and to cooperate with similar groups in other communions. By now a leading figure in the church, Vida Scudder was one of the two women appointed to this commission. She saw as its chief aim not "the undertaking of practical reforms which must in the nature of things lie outside its scope, but the social education of each communicant and each child of the Church."[3]

Scudder had just such a goal in mind when writing her book *Socialism and Character.* Very early in her career she had seen the economic reality of socialism. But how to reconcile the tenets of materialistic socialism with the spiritual message at the heart of Christianity was the problem she grappled with personally, even as she discussed the socialism of Christ or the relation of socialism to progress with Christian Socialist groups. Her own quest for inner unity forced her to face the doctrinal dilemmas she had skirted in these earlier writings. Years of reading, discussing, and prayerful meditation resulted in a doctrinal synthesis of Christian and socialist principles which quickened her own religious faith and led her inexorably to the still-difficult decision to join the Socialist Party.

The development of this synthesis was a gradual process, and in several lengthy articles Vida Scudder had tested some of these ideas. In 1909 she wrote a two-part essay for the *Hibbert Journal* on "The Social Conscience of the Future," followed a year later by "Christianity in the Socialist State." In 1910 she contributed "Religion and Socialism" to the *Harvard Theological Review*. Later that year, "Socialism and Sacrifice" appeared in the *Atlantic Monthly*, and in the following year the *Atlantic Monthly* carried her "Class Consciousness" and "Forerunners." These articles contained ideas difficult for the socially concerned Christian, as Vida Scudder well knew.[4] "I fought my way to my little red card through all these difficulties," she wrote later to Walter Rauschenbusch in commenting on his own work.[5]

## Socialism and Character

Shortly after she joined the Socialist Party Vida Scudder explored and developed these ideas in her book *Socialism and Character*. Although she later considered the book premature, she still felt it contained some of her best thinking. Here Vida Scudder took a personal approach, calling on her own background, to describe the experiences of modern Christians concerned with social issues, the ideals motivating them, the frustrations and the inevitable dilemmas that the reality of industrialism presented, before she moved on to a discussion of the major socialist tenets. The main thrust of the book focused on the issue raised years before by Ruskin, "whether the manufacture of souls of a good quality" was worthy of the attention of manufacturers and whether such a thing was possible under socialism.[6]

*Socialism and Character* is divided into four main parts, The Dilemma, First Principles, The Future of Character, and The Future of Religion. A careful review of the argument here will reveal the core of Scudder's socialist thought, which did not change substantially after this period, as well as the mental and spiritual struggle which preceded her full socialist commitment. More important is the strong Christian faith underlying this commitment which challenged and inspired so many of the future leaders of the Episcopal Church and the Socialist Party.

**Part I: The Dilemma.** At the outset Vida Scudder warned her reader that she was writing from the point of view of a "class-conscious, revolutionary socialist," and that she intended to discuss "the probable moral and spiritual results of the social change that seems to be impending" and to suggest ways to prepare the mind for these changes (5–7).

Scudder began with a review of the circumstances that led to the modern dilemma as she had experienced it, calling largely on the literary impulses she had discussed in *Social Ideals in English Letters*. The first reaction to the literary prophets of the nineteenth century resulted in a frenzy of philanthropy, followed closely by a zeal to reform society. By the twentieth century, idealists ruefully realized the futility of both paths. Since neither church nor society offered any guidance or encouragement, they looked again to the guides of their youth. Though they now perceived in literature a closer relation between the social and the spiritual, still the medley of solutions came to two—either moralize civilization or abandon it (9–28). Both had been tried and had failed. But idealists discovered a third force that had been evolving in reaction to the same set of circumstances. The same frustration with the inequities of the social system, the same yearning for fellowship with God and humanity seen in the literature of the nineteenth century, was evident in socialist writing. But socialism offered a third route: transform society, and used the new scientific language which alarmed both the religious and the industrial world. Instead of discussing the means of distributing wealth, socialists questioned the whole idea of property. In challenging the inalienable right to property, they had touched the very core of society. The other major tenet, class consciousness or the class struggle, was a practical means to the end, although it, too, had the ultimate goal of universal fellowship. But before going into a discussion of these two principle tenets of socialism, Scudder looked briefly at the modern aversions to socialism based on moral grounds.

Scudder distinguished three zones or levels of opposition to socialism in the early twentieth century. In the first, which she called *Prejudice*, were all those whose interests would suffer under a system of social equality. To the older socialists or the economic determinists of the cruder sort this was the only opposition that really counted, and it was against this group that they exerted their greatest effort. But to Scudder the spiritual dynamic was a more determining feature in impelling social change, and it was in that second region of *Appearances* that a deeper, nobler distrust obtained. Those who were concerned about the clash between clericalism and social democracy, those who were disturbed by the socialist disregard for eternal verities, those who were upset by the accidentals of socialism and knew little of the essentials of the socialist philosophy were in this group. As socialism matured and refined the crasser elements within and outside the movement, it would win the support of the idealists in this group. But in the third zone of *Realities* Scudder felt that the ultimate fate of the movement would be decided. On this level, ideas confronted each other "honest and unmasked." Socialism and religion, each stripped of prejudices and delusions, must determine whether they were essentially allied or fundamentally opposed (81–89). Scudder's argument in this book is directed toward the difficulties encountered at this level.

Religion, so opposed to socialism, was a major part of the dilemma. Its chief argument against socialism was that such a state would eliminate the very situations that have called forth from high-spirited men and women those heroic qualities so admired in the saints throughout the ages. To Scudder, such an apologia demanded the inequalities of privilege and provided no alternative to socialism. If religion would reveal the deeper meaning in this new historic development, as it had done so often in the past, it must make a thorough study of those principles, economic determinism and the class-struggle, and present a counter-philosophy (93–108).

**Part II: First Principles.** Scudder moved from this religious dilemma to a discussion of these two main principles, economic determinism and the class struggle, or class consciousness, as she preferred to call it. Scudder admitted the difficulty of reconciling her own ideals with the harder side of socialism. "The moments when two ideas, thought to be irreconcilable, are perceived to be supplementary, are the most radiant in one's inner history" (125), she wrote of her own final conversion. Here she intended to show that economic determinism was not an abandoning of spiritual ideals but an "eager appeal to social realities for guidance" in implementing those ideals (136). Again, she called on her own experience in reform organizations from the settlements to the labor unions. The impact of all of these on the workers was negligible compared to the impact of the economic facts—the hours they worked and the wages they received. Such experience forced Scudder to reexamine the assumptions on which she had been operating. She was not ready to abandon idealists like Ruskin and Tolstoy completely, but she did recognize that the solutions they plotted were divorced from the economic reality in which most people lived. On the contrary, realists like Bakunin saw that every great moral force arose out of common experience, out of the economic realities of the present age. Scudder believed that individuals still had a large part to play in shaping the world in which they lived, but to do this they must be in touch with the great economic forces at play. This call for a fusion of social idealism and economic determinism was as difficult for her radical socialist readers as for her more conservative Christian audience (132–36).

Scudder moved on to the second major principle of socialism, class consciousness, which followed from the first. Like Friedrich Engels, she accepted that view of history which saw the changing modes of production determining the division of classes. In the nineteenth century the industrial and political revolutions had given rise to a new working class. Socialists expected the next stage in that development to be the rise to conscious power of that class.

Scudder's concern was how that rise or advance was to be directed. Would it be left to the cruder socialist idea expressed in terms of hate? Would reformers continue to ignore movements arising from the people themselves?

In the early twentieth century two movements were developing this class consciousness, trade unionism and socialism. Although Scudder frequently criticized the limited vision of the trade unions, she admitted that, more than any other force, the unions had brought a unity of aim to the immigrant workers, and the labor struggles had produced in the workers those virtues of self-sacrifice and loyalty to a higher cause so often lacking in America.[7]

Socialism was not yet as strong as the union movement in America but it, too, was instilling in the people a sense of unity, a spirit of loyalty to the group, and a vision of a better world (162–63). These class struggles revealed a sense of dedication and disinterestedness that she did not see either in the unorganized or in the individual employees.[8]

She saw class consciousness as a special form of group consciousness that would divide humanity along horizontal rather than vertical lines, overcoming deep-seated antagonisms of race, nation, and religion. Yet, contrary to Marx or to Bakunin's view that socialism would do away with "the fatherland," or Herbert Croly's fear that socialism was a "menace to the national principle," Scudder felt that patriotism had "deep roots" and socialism would, in fact, supplement nationalism, (165–68), for most people were able to enjoy a multiplicity of loyalties.[9]

Class consciousness applied to the privileged class as well as to the unprivileged. Those who deplored working-class consciousness were often the most eager to foster such consciousness among their own. On the contrary, those who worked hardest for working-class solidarity hated class distinctions and saw the abolition of privilege as a means of ending all distinctions, said Scudder. With all distinctions or privileges gone, fears of a class war would disappear as well (168–73).

**Part III: The Future of Character.** In this book Scudder's main purpose was not to analyze the tenets of socialism but to consider the impact of such a society on character. Of one thing she was certain, character would have a determining influence on socialism. Unless socialism was prepared for by, or came as the result of, an "inward transformation," she warned, "it would prove the worst disaster of any experiment in collective living that the world has seen" (187). This conviction was behind her decision to join the Socialist Party as well as behind her zeal to win over prominent Christian leaders. She was even more determined to alert the Christian churches to their obligation to direct and shape the future in the light of the economic reality around them.[10]

Such an inner change was not the impossible dream. Scudder looked back over history and literature to show that such a transformation had accompanied every new social order. The self-regarding virtues of the present would yield to the new, as had happened before. Presuming the new age to be the socialist state, Scudder predicted certain aspects of that order (188–90). The most obvious modification would be in the realm of freedom. The socialist state would require an unprecedented discipline. For that reason alone it was important to stress both the evolutionary nature of socialism and the need to prepare for it. Unless the authority and discipline were a result of the enlightened will of the community it would be but tyranny. Therefore, the socialist state depended on the growth of democracy through generations to enlarge the meaning of freedom. By the time the socialist state arrived, this freedom would mean "the power bestowed by the community upon its every member to rise to the level of his richest capacity by living in harmony with the whole" (205). Some would chafe under these restrictions, some would suffer, but in comparison with the waste of the present system the surrender demanded from these would be negligible (193–205).

In two interesting chapters Scudder contrasted the ethics of a system based on social inequalities with that based on social equalities. The best qualities of the Haves were a result of the very conditions they deplored. Their finer virtues of mercy, pity, and generosity flourished in reform periods, but, according to Scudder, even the virtues themselves fared poorly at such times. Charity soon became cold and efficient, generosity seemed demoralizing, and the joy in giving turned to guilt feelings. Virtues of the Have-nots—meekness, purity of heart, and aspirations after justice—were hard to cultivate "in an unclean tenement on a starvation wage." The poverty of Christ and of all great religious thinkers Scudder defined as "a state of freedom from worldly interests," whereas industrial poverty was "a state of helpless bondage to these interests" (216–19). Attempts to follow the ideal of Christ as fully as possible had been no more successful among the spiritually elite, she pointed out, whether they sought personal perfection as did the Franciscans or social regeneration as did Tolstoy. The counsels of perfection would continue to attract, but they could never be a regenerative source so long as they ran counter to the very ideals society most cherished (233–237).

Scudder then considered the ethical situation that would prevail in a state based "on sustained equality of economic opportunity" (241). Here labor would be conscripted and assigned by an enlightened community, and the laborers' remuneration would be determined by scientific studies of the art of living. Under such conditions how would virtue fare? Charity would no longer mean a "money dole" but would assume again the definition of Saint Paul as a power "which forbears patiently, knows neither envy nor vanity, never tolerates bad manners, and rejoices only in the truth" (247). Socialism would not eliminate suffering, physical, mental, or spiritual, and there would still be room for compassion, chivalry, self-sacrifice. Even that "most aristocratic of virtues—a high magnanimous scorn of material rewards"—would be an attitude within the reach of all. And the virtues of the poor, obedience and submission, would be qualities highly regarded by all good socialists (252). Socialism would require a new art of living, and sympathy would help one to overcome antipathies, to be tolerant without being indifferent, to be generous and affectionate toward one another. In short, Scudder saw sympathy as another definition for that loyalty to the whole that was the end of socialism (256).

On the other hand, socialism was not the millenium. Men and women would not change. There might even be more wickedness in the socialist state where there was less moral confusion. A new

crop of hypocrisies might find rich opportunity in corporate industry. Purity might find survival difficult unless men and women
developed that "... social instinct which shrinks from sinning
against love, and then ... a ready submission to discipline and re-
straint which should be instinctive to the new citizen..." (259–
60).

As Scudder looked back over the centuries, she saw that the
highest virtue, like the highest genius, usually was found in conditions of reasonable economic security. Since these were the conditions that socialism hoped to make common, Scudder expected
that the spiritual as well as the cultural life would actually thrive
under socialism (262–64).

Scudder saw a new world evolving and hoped to see socialist
thought maturing. She recognized, too, that the socialist state
might be a "moral disaster," but if so, religion would have only
itself to blame for failing "to infuse its own dynamic into the
new order so evidently on the way, and to make socialism an expression of its own soul" (283).

Scudder was struck by the essentially conservative features of
socialism. Contrary to the view of most socialists and anti-socialists
as well, Scudder claimed that socialism was at its most conservative
in its attitude toward private property. She at this time agreed
with Leo XIII that property was an extension of personality, and
she went further and described it as "gauge and witness of our
fellowship with the Creator" (290). But the unchecked instinct
to accumulate was a perversion of this. It was this perversion that
Marx railed against in the *Communist Manifesto* when he pointed
out that a necessary condition for this privilege of the few was
the "non-existence of any property for the immense majority"
(292). Humanity had lost sight of its responsibility toward mother
earth, and Scudder again struck a distinctly modern note in in-
sisting on the need for all people to develop an impulse for stewardship that would be as successful along lateral lines as it had been
along hereditary lines. To socialists in 1912, one step in this direction was the socialization of all "wealth-producing wealth," (293)

which would in time distribute the fruits of the earth among the many, not just the few (285–98).

**Part IV: The Future of Religion.** In daring to discuss the future of religion in the socialist state Scudder attempted in the last section of her book what thirty years later would be called the Christian-Marxist dialogue. If avid socialists found her vague in discussion of socialist doctrine, philosophers and theologians found this section equally obscure. But here Scudder was writing out of the depths of her own soul-searching, agonizing attempt to reconcile these two opposing forces which together offered the best hope for the just society.

The socialist state was not committed to any one religion, but Scudder firmly believed that socialism would leave more scope for men and women to seek the ultimate truth than had previous social systems. Christianity was unique among all world religions because the distinctive feature, the very essence of Christianity, was the image of Jesus. Without going into the whole debate over the historical question, Scudder considered the concepts that preserved that image, the doctrine of the Trinity and the doctrines of the Incarnation and Atonement. These doctrines had special meaning for Christians who were socialists, for while they could not plumb the depths of the great mystery of the Trinity, they did assert in this mystery the faith that reality was found, "not in isolation, but in fellowship; not in self-seeking, but in a giving of self to the uttermost; not in personality shut in upon itself, but in an equal interchange of love attaining that highest unity which only differentiation can produce" (352).

Central also to Christianity but closer to the human experience was faith in the doctrine of the Incarnation and Atonement. The belief that the spirit could only be revealed through the flesh has led to the Christian demand for a just society that will allow the full emancipation of the higher life of the mind and spirit. Scudder felt the doctrine of Atonement was even more necessary to the socialist state. To her, the socialist state, like every new society, must be on guard against, sensitive to, its own moral failures. Yet it need not be afraid to measure itself against the ideal, for Christianity showed the Supreme Judge as Redeemer as well, a Redeemer who worked not through "isolated miracles" but with and through all those who sacrificed themselves for the world's need in a spirit of penitence (363–65).

Scudder felt that Christianity was the religion best suited to a state that placed such emphasis on historical fact, both as an interpretation of the past and as a guide to social advance. Although socialism and Catholicism were at the time bitter opponents, Scudder nevertheless considered Catholicism "a more social form of Christianity" and "more likely than Protestantism to adapt itself to the socialized state". Catholicism subordinated yet deepened the individual life and called for restraints in harmony with the discipline of the socialized state. Its emphasis on tradition, she felt, made Catholicism the most truly progressive force, for "nothing can grow that is not rooted." In its sacramental system, in its call for sacrifice, in its hold on the secret of Jesus, in its belief in a revelation of "absolute though unfolding truth," the Catholic Church would best meet the needs of the socialized state. No doubt the church, too, would have to undergo great changes to meet the demands of the new society and Vida Scudder rejoiced in the thought that "the agony of inward transformation" was already in process in the church (361–71).

Scudder never claimed Jesus was a socialist, but to her mind He did implant an ideal animating all human progress; thus Christianity led directly to socialism. Though she was greatly influenced by the thought of Walter Rauschenbusch, Scudder did not equate the socialist state with the Kingdom. The evolutionary process in nature and in society would continue, and leaders in the coming socialist state would have a further vision. Another constant theme in Scudder's book is that of loyalty. Scudder showed the influence of Josiah Royce, who wrote often of Loyalty of the Whole and of the problem of Community, which were dominant themes in Scudder's writing in these years. Although she so often used Royce's phraseology, Scudder attributed her own understanding of loyalty to Saint Catherine of Siena.[11]

## Chapter Five

# Impact of the War Years

## The Church and Socialism

**The Lawrence Strike.**    Shortly after *Socialism and Character* appeared, The Progressive Women's Club of Lawrence, Massachusetts, asked Vida Scudder to address a meeting of the women called to protest police brutality in connection with the strike in the Lawrence textile mills. The strike was then in its third month and national attention was focused on Lawrence. On Sunday, March 3, 1912, Scudder and her Wellesley colleague Ellen Hayes visited Lawrence to meet some of the women involved in the incidents with the police and to ascertain firsthand the mood in the city. The following evening she introduced herself to the meeting as an outsider who, despite the conflicting testimonies of the situation in Lawrence, felt the necessity of bearing witness to great principles. Continuing with the words, "Blessed are ye when men shall revile you and persecute you," she presented her carefully thought-out and precisely worded position. Whether the strike was "for justice sake" or not, certain ends of justice were obviously being achieved. She praised especially the work of the Strike Committee presided over by Joseph Ettor of the International Workers of the World, although the strike was not under IWW auspices. The Committee itself, composed of several organizations and at least eighteen nationalities, represented fraternity and hope to her, for "on every man and woman there had flashed the vision of a just society, based on fair reward to labor and on fraternal peace." It was fear of just such "fraternity" that struck terror into the hearts of conservatives and progressive reformers alike and was behind strident demands for immigration restriction in New England. Scudder was well aware of this, if her listeners were not, and her theme had been chosen designedly.[1]

For the two professors the repercussions were stronger in Boston than in Lawrence. The *Boston Evening Transcript* denounced the Wellesley professors for spreading radical doctrine and demanded their resignation from Wellesley College. The *Transcript* was especially vehement toward Scudder. Letters poured into the administration at Wellesley, and she was again asked to explain her position to the Board of Trustees. Scudder admitted that she was a member of the Socialist Party, that her sympathies were with the conservative wing of the Party which repudiated violence, and referred them to her book, *Socialism and Character,* as representing as clearly as she could her present views. No resignations were asked for, but Scudder was asked to drop her course "Social Ideals in English Letters" for the following year. Years later Scudder recalled that though her friendship with Katherine Lee Bates, head of the English department, endured the strain, she felt that her colleague "never again quite trusted [her] classroom judgment."[2]

**Socialist and Churchwoman.** The experience of that year convinced Scudder more than ever of the need for a more radical witness in the church and in the community. She was disappointed, but not surprised, that so few of the settlement workers had supported the strike in Lawrence. In May she resigned as head of the Italian Committee at Denison House, for she knew her political views were a cause of concern and tension. However, she still continued to serve on the executive committee of the settlement and promoted the interests of the College Settlements Association on college campuses.

That fall she and her mother moved to Wellesley, and she determined to take a more active role in the life of the college. Undisturbed by the Wellesley authorities, she lectured frequently for the Intercollegiate Socialist Society on New England college campuses. The need to educate church leaders to their social responsibilities was even more pressing, and she contributed to a variety of religious and socialist periodicals, referring to herself now as a socialist churchwoman. She insisted to men like Walter Rauschen-busch that party membership was vitally important if they really desired a "political socialism of a better type." The substance of his negative reply can be conjectured from her letter a few weeks later absolving him but stating frankly "that a man of your acknowl-edged status as a sane and spiritual leader should have to plead worldly prudence as one factor in his decision is a tragic reflection on the modern Church."[3]

She was disappointed, too, that close friends like Jane Addams and Helena Dudley could not accept her socialist views. However, she realized that there was much more "intellectual travail" re-quired in becoming a Socialist than in becoming a Republican or a Democrat, and in her view the Progressive platform was "hardly more than an orderly expression of goodwill angered by our obvious social wrongs." To become a Socialist even intellectually involved "an abandonment of traditions instinctively cherished," and she was more patient with the faint-hearted than with the prudent. In the Party she saw her role as doctrinal synthesizer and educator as well, and she did not hesitate to blame the socialist concentration on the material for the polarization of views between Socialists and concerned church people.[4]

*The Church and the Hour.* This "propaganda on two sides" can best be seen in her book, *The Church and the Hour: Reflections of a Socialist Churchwoman,* which is a reprint of representative lec-tures and articles written during these immediate prewar years. Whether intended originally for church leaders as was the opening essay, "The Alleged Failure of The Church to Meet the Social Emer-gency," or for confirmed Socialists, as was her article, "Why Does Not The Church Turn Socialist," all the papers were originally pre-sented and collected here for the express purpose of promoting "bet-ter understanding between the religious world which fears social revolution and the unchurched world of radical passion which desires it."[5] In the first essay mentioned above Scudder rebutted many of the criticisms of the church, describing it as an "interpenetrating force" rather than a separate body (45). As such, it should have no stand on single tax, socialism, or syndicalism, but the members had an obliation to use their Christian ideals to evaluate these proposals (48–53). She admitted a general uneasiness about the increasing divisions between "spiritual and social Christianity," which to her were two vital aspects of the one Christian inheritance. In fact, she saw an intimate union between "the Catholic faith at its fullest and social radicalism at its boldest" (66–69). To the largely socialist readers of the *The Coming Nation* she approached the same issues but in a different tone. The church should not be considered as "one corporate being endowed with independent life," she wrote, and should not be expected to identify itself with any political or economic "system" (105–106). The real question was why so few members of the church joined the Socialist Party. She answered this frankly. Even the most committed Christian Socialist found it difficult to dispel the fear of a lack of moral and spiritual values which socialism conveyed to the more socially concerned Christians. Socialists had an obligation here. She saw "no logical reason why socialists should not care for spiritual values, and religious people care for social justice. . . . neither cause can in the long run flourish without the other" (117–18). In the concluding essay in the book, "A Plea for Social Intercession" from *The Churchman,* Scudder called on all the churches to turn again to the prayer of intercession which she defined as the "counterpart in the life within of social work in the life without" (123). Intercessory prayer was an integral part of the prayer life of members of the Church Socialist League and of the Society of the Companions of the Holy Cross, and Scudder, who greatly influenced both groups, saw this prayer as a powerful means readily available to the churches to make people aware of the social message of the Gospel. If the church taught people to be honest in prayer, to energize their life of prayer, to be intelligent about social issues, then what forces for social justice would follow (126–30).

## The Doubting Pacifist

*Le Morte d'Arthur.*   For many years Scudder had been teaching courses on Arthurian Romance, and her medieval spirit revelled in it. In 1917 she published *Le Morte d'Arthur of Sir Thomas Malory,* which she dedicated to the publisher, James M. Dent, now a devoted friend and admirer. This book proved to herself and her critics her ability to do sustained scholarly research and to communicate her keen analytical observations in a direct and lucid style. *Le Morte d'Arthur* reveals her deep love and wide knowledge of medieval life and literature and met with much more positive criticism from reviewers than did her writings of a religious or social nature. This book was more than a detailed study of parallel sources of the Arthurian legend. Before discussing the sources, Scudder gave a necessary introduction to the entire subject of the Arthurian legend and then showed the superiority of Malory's use of these sources and traditions to produce his famous *Le Morte d'Arthur.* Although stressing the artistic treatment of the work, Vida Scudder emphasized its significance as a social document as well. The dominating trait of the Middle Ages to her was loyalty, and in *Le Morte d'Arthur* she saw loyalty to God, to lord, and to lady growing into that loyalty to the whole so necessary for a truly unified state. As in the literature of the earlier ages, she saw here, too, Christianity challenging men to "follow its own uncompromising standard" until "its own vision [became] the normal one."[6]

**"The Doubting Pacifist."** Loyalty again became a vexing problem for Vida Scudder herself in the next few years. Scudder had never written seriously about the question of war or peace and like most progressives felt war was an anachronism. Unlike most of her settlement colleagues in New England, she had seen in the varieties of people coming to America the best hope for international understanding. Years before she had been stunned by the role of the United States in the Spanish-American war, just when she felt the country was moving in a positive direction. A few years earlier she had questioned the advances made by civilizations such as the United States and Great Britain that justified their wars in the Philippines and in Africa as being for the ultimate good of the enemy. But in 1914 conditions in the United States and in the world seemed so grave that she confessed a "certain horrified relief when war broke out." Reformers, radicals, and peace advocates were sharply divided over the role of the United States. Scudder felt socialists should be in the front row of pacifists if this were their belief. She herself could not accept absolute pacifism or nonresistance.

Engaged as she was in her study of *Le Morte d'Arthur,* she felt wars of chivalry, to defend weaker states or in self-defense, were at times necessary, and nonresistance was a counsel for an individual, not the state.[7] Speaking in 1916 at a Congress of the Protestant Episcopal Church in Norfolk, Virginia, she not only opposed preparedness but went further, saying that unless some nation was willing "to offer itself as a martyr and move to disarmament" peace would never come to the world.[8] Still, she was not a pacifist. In 1917, although she saw the defeat of Germany as a "stern necessity," she still opposed conscription as an attempt to fasten a "military machine on the country just when we were entering a war with the ostensible purpose of destroying forever the need for such machines."[9] These utterances were indeed confusing. Because she was a socialist and so outspoken in her defense of civil liberties, Scudder was often considered a pacifist. But this was a position she could not accept although her closest friends were pacifists. From Scudder's summer home in Shelburne, New Hampshire, her good friend Helena Dudley, a pacifist, wrote to Jane Addams, now President of the Women's International League for Peace and Freedom, of the tensions that existed still between herself and Scudder on this issue.[10] Even Scudder's radical socialist friends found it difficult to agree with her view that pacifism was a disavowal of the class war.[11]

Her only lengthy discussion of pacifism at this time is in "The Doubting Pacifist" in the *Yale Review.* Here she questioned the "troubling materialism" in the pacifist belief that the taking of human life was the "supreme wrong" because it destroyed personality. Surely some pacifists still believed in eternal life and understood Christ's teaching that those who had power to kill the body were not the final arbiters of human destiny. To her, the industrial conditions devastating human souls were a far greater evil and struck just as surely at the roots of personality. She criticized the pacifists, therefore, for not connecting war with "the conflicting interests" which were "the ruling principles of the economic order," and for not moving toward a more "constructive social radicalism" which would link "war into the whole causal circle where it [belonged]" (742–43).

At the same time Scudder vigorously defended the pacifist's right to dissent. She warned her fellow Americans against the danger of the "invasion of our own natures and our own country by the very evils which we attack" and almost prophetically described the evils of intolerance that would come in the aftermath of war (748–49, 751). Within a few months that evil spirit of intolerance invaded even the institutions closest to Scudder. Emily Greene Balch, head of the economics department at Wellesley, had become deeply involved in the peace movement during a leave of absence, and the question of her reappointment in 1918 was tied in with the question of loyalty. Writing to offer Balch her support Scudder confessed that she was on the defensive "and rather bewildered to be for once on the majority side, really a little disgraced."[12]

A similar situation arose in the ranks of the hierarchy of the Episcopal Church when the Right Reverend Paul Jones, Bishop of Utah, was allowed to resign because of protests against his pacifist and socialist views.[13] In Scudder's view, both Balch and Jones represented the true socialist position. Loyalty to the larger whole obliged each to take a stand opposed to that of the majority in the more immediate group. Although she personally felt that pacifists, once war was declared, could find more constructive employment than denouncing the war in progress, nevertheless Scudder insisted that whenever the socialist mind disapproved, "opposition should continue openly and with dignity. This for the sake of true national honour, compromised when a nation makes a false choice." Convinced that this freedom or loyalty to conscience was essential in a democratic and socialist state, Scudder, in the face of mounting intolerance in the country, was constant in her efforts at all levels in behalf of men like Eugene Debs, Victor

Berger, Tom Mooney, and others who were imprisoned for religious or social convictions. As a result she often had to defend
herself against charges of pacifism.[14]

The impact of the thought and writing of such people as
Scudder did help to reshape pacifist thought. Shortly after the war
the Fellowship of Reconciliation recognized that violence was
implicit in the present unjust social order and geared itself to work
for constructive social change. Scudder was eager to join then, for
this involved no compromise with her belief that coercion might
indeed be necessary to bring about social change. Helena Dudley,
an early member of this Fellowship, was now ready to accept Scudder's socialist position.[15] In the inter-war years the Fellowship of
Reconciliation was the most radical pacifist group. In the next decade Scudder continued to wrestle with pacifism and communism.
Her views on pacifism changed dramatically, shaped by the religious
and economic upheavals of those tumultuous years.

## The Social Teachings of the Christian Year

In 1918 Vida Scudder gave a series of lectures at the Episcopal
Theological School in Cambridge; they were revised and published
in 1921 as *The Social Teachings of the Christian Year.* Directed
to those who followed the Christian year through the liturgy of
the Anglican Prayer Book, the lectures reveal the deep, almost
mystical faith of Scudder which was the basis and support of her
socialist commitment and which softened even her most extrava-
gant views. Scudder saw worship as the center of the life of the
church and the gradual enrichment of the liturgy, the visible
expression of this worship over the years, was the purest expression
of "organic human fellowship" which Christianity presented.[16]
Simply by moving prayerfully through the liturgical seasons, Christians, with a little guidance, developed a social discipline and became aware of the social, even revolutionary implications of the
Gospel message as presented in the liturgical year from Advent to
Trinitytide. In these lectures Scudder shared the fruits of her own
contemplation with such fervor that she was in the next decade

the spiritual leader and guide of many socially concerned and socialist-oriented young clergy.

Advent had a threefold social message—Change, the Kingdom, and Judgment. Each week in the Advent season the church recalled a special coming or fulfillment with its special warning, and always the emphasis was social as well as personal. Just so, the response of the Christian must be social as well as personal. The more one entered into the spirit of the liturgy, the less one feared the changes that must come in both personal and social relations (16–20). In the same way the message of the Kingdom would go beyond the idea of the interior kingdom to a broader view of a social order based on justice and love. To Scudder, the Advent liturgy taught that catastrophe was not necessarily disaster, nor was tranquillity always a blessing. The Christian must not then condemn wars or revolutions simply because they were destructive, for these might be preordained signs. On the other hand, Christians must try to avert disaster. The time of preparation was not a time of fear or of passivity but a time of hope. To Scudder, the liturgy taught that the times of judgment were the "Springtides of the World" (29–32).

Scudder found the message of each season carried into the next and further developed in the light of each new revelation. At Christmas judgment gave way to contemplation of the great mystery of the Word made Flesh and living in this world. The social implications were many but none so clear as the dependence of the Christ Child on others. So all work done for the dependent, a vital part of Christian tradition, was sanctified by the Incarnation (47–54). The Epiphany liturgy broadened the ideal of fellowship presented in the Christmas season. Labor, noted Vida Scudder, was fittingly the first at the Manger, but Wisdom followed closely. This "inclusiveness" of the Christian mystery was the keynote of the season, and "the fellowship of the Mystery" became the hallmark of the first community. The greatest barrier to the growth of the Kingdom, the spiritual order which Christ came to establish, was, in the eyes of Vida Scudder, the separateness among people and nations (67–69).

The season of Septuagesima was a transitional period between the joys of Christmastide and the penitential season of Lent. To Vida Scudder it was significant that the Church opened the season with the great parable of justice. The parable of the workers in the vineyard she termed the "trade-union" parable, but Scudder carried the message beyond that of the unions. Should not the true Christian society consider man not in the light of the past but of the future, supply him not on the basis of "what he has earned, but what will best enable him to develop a richer manhood?" (92–93).

Vida Scudder believed that no experience was "so private as penitence," yet no season was so social as Lent. To her, sin was a grim reality, however unfashionable at times, and the real war against evil had to be fought "on the battleground of personality" (107–9). For this reason, as the Lenten liturgy began, the readings showed the prophets denouncing not Israel's enemies but her own failings. Israel must assume responsibility for social injustice by social penitence and expiation. It was in this need for social reconstruction that the modern church had failed to learn from the prophets, had failed to offer challenging leadership, said Scudder (111–17).

The message of the Crucifixion was not simply endurance or passive acquiescence in suffering "but defiance of the existing social and religious order," of the sin which caused pain. This defiance or resistance was the keynote, the challenge of the liturgy for Holy Week: "Let this mind be in you which was also in Christ Jesus" (140–48).

The Easter liturgy made Vida Scudder acutely conscious "of the worthlessness of the Social Gospel without the spiritual." In the immediate triumph of immortality the group life was for once secondary, and the most intimate revelations of Jesus were individual. In each person's search for God there was a special union that was not shared with a group but was reserved for each individual. Yet the liturgy, after pointing out these special unions, returned again to the ethical messages of Christ rather than dwelling on the ecstasy of the Resurrection (163–66).

The first outpouring of the Spirit broke down the barriers among classes and people, and immediately the community of Christians reached out beyond its own confines. Within a short time the Church had become an international institution, but the struggle between nationalism and internationalism continued to blur the vision of unity (196–200). Similarly, the first impulse of the early Church was for a community of goods. That experiment, too, was brief but the ideal continued to permeate Christianity. Though the church did not enjoin voluntary poverty, to Scudder it was significant that the liturgical cycle each year challenged Christians to examine their attitude toward property (201–9).

In her earlier writings Scudder had emphasized that the church was larger than any "ism". Now, moved by events in Europe and especially in Russia, she felt that the church, too, would soon have to declare itself for or against the socialist movement. Christians, she felt, could transform the revolutions in progress, indeed they must. "Does it mean nothing that our Whitsun Altars glow with red? Might not the Red Flag find itself at home there?" she queried (210–14). Certainly Scudder was becoming more revolutionary in these immediate postwar years. But she was not so optimistic as she sounded. The red flag hung beside the crucifix in her own private oratory.[17] The continuing revolutions in postwar Europe, the struggles of President Woodrow Wilson for a League of Nations, were portents of a future soon to come. Now was the time to push for the completion of that industrial democracy advanced during the war years, but the reactionary forces in in the United States were gaining in strength. To forestall such reaction in the church, Scudder opened discussions that led to the formation of the Church League for Industrial Democracy (CLID) in 1919.[18] By 1922 CLID had attracted most of the leaders of the Church Socialist League. Scudder's role as chairperson of the executive committee of CLID was largely promotional and inspirational but vital to CLID in its early days. She herself had been extremely interested in the Russian experiment, but by the end of the 1920s she realized the folly of expecting any revolution that did not proceed "from a Christian conception of man" to provide a solution for social ills. But the relationship between religion and revolutionary change was still important, and she began to look for a meeting ground between Christianity and communism.[19]

## Chapter Six

# Franciscan Adventures

Saint Francis of Assisi has always had a special attraction for Christians, a romantic appeal for those who need heroes to idealize rather than imitate, the ultimate challenge for those who believe the Gospel message is meant to be fully lived. Scudder's devotion to Saint Francis went back to the early years of her career. The difficulty of trying to live a life moving in several different directions at once resulted in a serious break in her health early in 1901. That summer leisurely travel in Italy brought her, like most pilgrims and tourists, to Assisi. At the Hotel Subasio she had the good fortune to be seated at dinner opposite Paul Sabatier, the noted Franciscan scholar. Next to him an Anglican clergyman, a "Christian Tory," spoke in praise of modern philanthropy and the growth in charity toward the poor. Assisi had already cast its spell and Vida Scudder startled the two gentlemen with her vehement interjection: "We do not owe the poor charity; we owe them expiation." The intensity of the young American's remark attracted Sabatier. After dinner, from the balcony of the hotel, Monsieur Sabatier took her on a visual pilgrimage of the places sacred to the memory of Francis. To that night she traced her vocation to try to relate the history and teaching of the *Poverello* to modern needs.[1]

For over twenty years now she had worked tirelessly in that cause. These postwar years were discouraging times for all radicals, and Scudder looked forward to a well-earned sabbatical in 1922. Her letter to Ellen Gates Starr summed up her attitude at the time and her wiser assessment of this period as a breathing spell: "Perhaps we have a right, you and I, at our age, to cultivate a sense of perspective, and I find myself really more excited in digging myself into connections with the spiritual Franciscans through the obstructions of very solid Latin, than in fighting for modern reforms. But you know there always will be that second wind, or the third or the fourth; it is perhaps waiting for both of us." On her return to Wellesley for the last lap of her teaching career, she continued her work on the Franciscans and during these years also wrote one of her favorite books, *Brother John*.[2]

### Brother John

In the early 1900s Scudder had been so immersed in the letters of Saint Catherine that her novel, *The Disciple of a Saint*, had almost written itself. Now, as she explored the early struggle of the Franciscans, *Brother John* emerged as the companion piece. All the good causes she had supported for so long were on the defensive in the 1920s, and Scudder readily identified with the besieged friars. *Brother John* allowed her imagination more play than the historical study she was then preparing, and the problems facing the friars in the early years of the order have a perennially modern ring.

On Christmas Eve young John of Sanfort, heir to a great name and fortune in Cornwall, England, disturbed by the contrast between the feasting in the castle and the poverty of the manger, fled to the woods. Here he met two of the Little Brothers and abandoned wealth and position to follow them. John soon found himself embroiled in the internal struggles of the young order. At Oxford he became an intimate of the leading English Franciscans and accompanied the delegation sent to Rome to oppose the worldly Minister–General Elias. The journey took them through Paris where John met the learned men of the order, and en route to Italy he was fortunate enough to see some of the giants who had lived with Francis. Characters familiar to lovers of Franciscan history and legend move easily in and out of the story as John tries to discover the true meaning of Francis and some understanding of the controversies shaking the order. Elias was deposed but the controversy continued, for there was a far deeper disunity among the friars than at first appeared. John realized he must make a decision, and despite his love and admiration for the English friars he cast his lot with the spirituals or zealots. Such a choice meant that he would never again be able to serve the order he loved so well, but he could do no other. The real spirit of "Naughting," of "Nichilitade," had captivated him. But not until his final years did John learn that the struggle to live the ideal of Saint Francis, yet to remain in the world, difficult as it was, was not so difficult as the final stage of that "Naughting," the absence of confidence, the doubt, the fear that one had not understood the message aright. These were the fears that assailed John as he lay dying, imprisoned the previous five years by the Minister–General Bonaventura for his part in the publication of a book considered dangerous. These were the doubts that ushered him into that "lowest depth of Naughting," the state he had yearned for but hesitated before for so long (307–8).

*Brother John* is more a spiritual romance based on historical incidents than a historical novel. The author herself forestalled certain criticisms by explaining in her introduction that John was in a feeble state when recalling the events of his youth. The reader is warned that John's assessments of some of the characters are his personal impressions of the brothers. The plot is simple, just enough to carry the characters and elucidate the controversy. The story was written for an audience that would not work its way through the more scholarly *Franciscan Adventure*, but the controversy is clearer here, certainly more poignant, and the transfer to the contemporary scene much more obvious. The hero in the story is again the mouthpiece of Vida Scudder voicing her beliefs, her dilemmas. Occasionally these become more important than the story, eclipsing the character who must have been formed in the struggle to decide.

John, the only fully imaginary character in the novel, is the least convincing. Rufino, Adam Marsh, Ayman, and Bernard are much more colorful, more carefully drawn, and as appealing as in the legends, no doubt because they are so real to Scudder. Franciscan scholars questioned her idea that the lauds or poems of Jacopone da Todi, who does not appear in the story or in Franciscan history until much later, were part of a growing mystic tradition in the order. Scudder was following her evolutionary approach to literature here, as anyone familiar with her *Social Ideals in English Literature* realized. (In *Socialism and Character* she argued that socialism was not necessarily the ideal economic or political philosophy but the next stage in man's continuing search for the ideal.) Although her *Franciscan Adventure* offered neither proof nor suggestion that Jacopone da Todi was putting into literary form ideas passed on from the early friars, she set forth that notion in the novel, more in response to her own mystical nature than to the facts (viii). Notwithstanding, the historical flaws are minor and detract little, if at all, from the story.[3]

Like *A Listener in Babel* and *The Disciple of a Saint*, *Brother John* is often autobiographical, though Scudder avoided many of the pitfalls of these earlier works. In *A Listener in Babel* the real-life counterparts of the fictional characters can almost be named. In both *A Listener in Babel* and *The Disciple of a Saint* characters whose views she did not agree with were straw figures, whereas in *Brother John* she showed much more sympathy for the English intellectuals and the moderates though the spirituals were unquestionably her favorites. But now at age 65, completing almost forty years of teaching and reform work, Scudder's answers to vital questions were not so clear-cut. She also understood much more clearly Francis's fear of learning, which led to "power" or to as many "uncontrollable wants" as did property or money. Certainly, too, she knew the struggles and doubts of the intellectuals with whom she felt she had cast her lot. Unlike Hilda in *A Listener in Babel*, John realized the full impact of his decision for himself and for his order, so he did not embark on this major step with the same exuberance as Hilda.

Ellen Gates Starr made several penetrating comments in her letter to Scudder about the book. Starr did not feel sufficiently well acquainted with the sources to review the book, but she found it a sad story despite Scudder's frequent reference to the great joy of the friars. Scudder focused so on the dilemma facing the friars that their joyous spirit did not come through. Starr made a still more telling point. For her, the book failed, not because of its sad over-tone but because the reader remained uncertain of the author's view—not whether the spirituals would succeed or not succeed, but whether they were right. "You don't know yourself, do you, dear?" she remarked, parenthetically.[4]

Scudder made several attempts to make the story relevant to her day, but she was true to the Franciscan sources and did not attempt to see their movement as social criticism. The truth of the book was that it showed clearly the real message of Francis. It was not what one did but what one was that mattered, and this was seen by the life one lived. Real joy went deeper than the senti-mental virtue of much popular Franciscan literature; in that deeper sense *Brother John* was not a sad book to Scudder. The hostility aroused by the spirituals seemed to her to witness to the righteous-ness of their position, nor did this hostility ever touch the inner peace of the friars, the source of true joy. The very hostility testified or witnessed to the validity of their cause.

## The Franciscan Adventure

In 1928 Vida Scudder retired from Wellesley College. Scudder was a brilliant, popular teacher, and though always troubled by the contrast between the life of privilege which she led and the classless society which she preached, she thoroughly enjoyed the intellectual challenge of students, scholarly exchange among fac-ulty, and the consternation of the administration at her radicalism. Perhaps it was that "second wind" she sensed when she wrote to Louise Hodgkins, a former head of the English department, of the excitement she felt at the prospect "of [picking] up the threads where [she] had dropped them at twenty-seven."[5] The first of these threads was her research and writing. Scudder was eager to resume work on her Franciscan history, in the first extended period of uninterrupted writing in forty-one years! After a summer spent partly in Shelburne and at Adelynrood, she set out for Assisi, accompanied by Florence Converse.

This visit to Italy was saddened by news of the death of Paul

Sabatier in France. Over the years an intimate friendship with the scholar and his wife had developed. Now the hills spoke of him and of the great devotion his work had inspired in so many others. His death brought still another boon to Scudder's work. Sabatier had wished his excellent library to go to the United States. Through her influence the treasures of his Franciscan collection were acquired by the Boston Public Library. The last stages of her *Franciscan Adventure* benefitted from her careful study of Sabatier's later work, which had shown a change from the ultra-Protestant approach in his *Vie de Saint François d'Assise* published in 1894.[6]

As a young teacher-writer, her good friend Katharine Lee Bates had warned her that her social involvement was detrimental to her career as a writer. It was a sacrifice the young teacher had made generously, and there was as much truth in the criticism as heroism in the final decision. When James M. Dent, her friend and publisher, wrote to her in 1919 that she should now devote herself to literary work, the same commitment, if not the same enthusiasm, was in her reply: "One must not do the congenial thing, one must work at the chores that seem to be appointed." Now at last she had time to give wholeheartedly to her writing. *The Franciscan Adventure* vindicated the judgment of her critic-friends and was her finest achievement.[7] For over twenty-five years she had been reading the history and literature of the period, and frequent trips to Italy had given her the opportunity to work with a variety of sources as well as to imbibe a feeling for and intimacy with the saints. *The Franciscan Adventure* shows a sure grasp of the spirit of the times and an able and careful handling of the sources from papal bulls to intimate legends of the Little Friars.

**Part I: The Background.** *The Franciscan Adventure* is not a history of the order, but a history of the struggle over the interpretation of Francis's Rule and Will that wracked the friars in the first stormy century following the death of the Founder. In her introduction Scudder quoted Sabatier's hope that one day a historian trained also as a sociologist and philosopher would study Saint Francis's concept of property.[8] In fact, over the years in her lectures and writings she had been trying to help modern man see the implications for contemporary society of Francis's life and Rule. Now was the time to examine his Rule from a new viewpoint and to see wherein it applied to society as a whole, not just to the individual.

Her history was carefully constructed. Part I traced the background out of which came the Franciscan movement. The monastic revivals from Augustine to Bernard showed the continual need for reform in the Church and the constant stirring of Christian souls to escape the trammels of the world. But these reforms scarcely touched the social or religious life of the ordinary people, and by the eleventh and twelfth centuries the individual reformers and numerous confraternities were proof of the needs of these common people for the same spiritual help. These groups, whether heretical or orthodox, were precursors of the mendicants and in a sense prepared the way for the radicalism of the Franciscans. These confraternities sprang directly from the poorer classes or "proletariat," as Scudder called them. The members of the confraternities did not choose poverty but, having it thrust upon them, made a virtue of necessity and saw poverty as a means of union with Christ. In contrast, most of the followers of Francis would never in private life have known poverty, and they embarked on their quest with a gaiety not seen before. The idea that a friar had to be well-born, else where was the sacrifice, was soon generally accepted. Scudder seems to agree, revealing the inconsistency in her own life and thought. Here is the subtle suggestion that the friars operated from a higher motive than did the members of the confraternities who, of course, did not have that hurdle of "privilege" to surmount, who could not pay the high cost of material renunciation.[9]

A more important contrast was the loyalty to the Catholic Church and obedience to priests that distinguished Francis and his followers from these other groups and was one explanation for the endurance of Francis's movement. Francis feared dangers to orthodoxy more than to poverty in his freedom-loving followers. Scudder pointed out that in both his Rule and his Will Francis reiterated his plea for obedience to the Church. Scudder had not agreed with Sabatier's earlier suggestion that Francis was a forerunner of the Reformation, and so she was fortunate to have access to his later work in which he had modified his interpretation.[10] Franciscan orthodoxy was combined with such spontaneity that the friars avoided the "subservient psychology" of the monk, she observed, again showing some of her Protestant prejudice which several of her reviewers noted (41–42).

Social criticism was not the purpose of Saint Francis. His emphasis was on life itself and the importance of living life to the full. His friends and followers spoke of Francis as "Innovator," and there was a disconcerting element in his life not readily understood even then. Those who would follow him must be content to live as "strangers and pilgrims" and not look for the security or stability of a monastic order. This radiance continued to attract men down the years, but how many of those who recognized the injustices in modern industrial capitalism were ready to see Francis as a "pioneer in protest against the wage system" or to recognize that the "spiritual vocation of the few might suggest a social principle to govern the many"? Neither, she admitted, did Saint Francis (58–59). However Scudder did intend to look for ways in which this ideal could apply to society, and this very open application to a socialist creed caused considerable consternation. Even those of Scudder's socialist persuasion might have preferred to be allowed to make these obvious applications themselves. Years of teaching and preaching no doubt were hard to shrug off.

**Part II: The Story.**   After this short digression Scudder moved into the heart of her story and focused on the struggle that threatened to disrupt the Franciscan movement in the thirteenth century. She placed Francis against the background of political intrigue and commercial greed in Italy where a rising merchant-class struggled against the controls of Pope and emperor to emphasize the fact that Francis's dread of money, his understanding of the relationship between property and war, were not theoretical but experiential (68–69).

Scudder was not writing another life of Saint Francis, and she moved along immediately to the years from the first approval of his Rule in 1223 to the final attempt by Pope John XXII in 1323 to solve the controversy by declaring heretical the teaching on the Poverty of Christ which was central to the life of the monastic orders and the very heart of all Franciscans. Yet the Poverello's spirit fills every page of the book, and this is the charm of the story, bitter though it is, as told by Scudder. Scudder focused completely on the internal struggles of the friars in the period that was at the same time marked by the greatest growth and achievements of the order. Most of the trouble centered around the Rule and Last Will of Francis, and Scudder went into detail here. Even the reader not too familiar with the early history of the order, carried along by the enthusiasm of the author, could follow this exposition with interest. Francis had some doubts about the concessions he had made in this third will, which still prohibited the ownership of land or houses and any dealing with money. Therefore, before he died he wrote his Last Will which he ordered to be read weekly by the friars and which explicitly stated his intention.

From the time of his death, debate began on the obligation of friars to the Will and to the Rule. As the order grew, so did the difficulties involved in living either the Rule or the Will, and the friars made frequent appeals to Rome. The papal bull "Quo Elongati" in 1230 attempted to solve the dilemma by exempting the friars from literal obedience to the Will and allowing the use of goods held in trust for them by a lay person. The first Minister-General John Parente resigned in this struggle and a stronger leader was appointed in Elias. But strong leadership was resented, too. Elias was eventually deposed not for his luxurious life-style as is so often noted, but for his autocratic handling of affairs and his preference for the lay rather than the clerical element (94–97). In the years following Elias, the basic disunity of mind among the friars was revealed, and Francis's great fear regarding love of learning among his friars was vindicated. The order moved quickly from a "spontaneous lay fellowship into an order of clerks or priests" marked by their great love of learning (102–6). The time would soon be ripe for the great Bonaventura.

Scudder interrupted her narrative to reflect on the great "release of life" in the first half century of the Franciscans, the contributions to art, music, architecture, and learning, not to slight the works of mercy to which a great number of Franciscans dedicated themselves. All this while the conflict over the application of the ideal of Francis to the contemporary world waged within the order. The Popes were always favorable to the order and as anxious to preserve the ideal of Francis as they were to concede to the frailties of his followers and to avoid the threats to an ordered society that radical Franciscanism implied. As learning increased so did exemptions, but the zealots or spirituals continued to prick the conscience of friars. Time and again recourse was made to the Pope to clarify or justify their attitude toward property. As Francis realized, learning with all the paraphernalia it required was inconsistent with the free love of vagabondage he enjoined. As Scudder pointed out, once the practice of the virtues was conditioned by the work of the friars, rather than the vows determining the kind of work they would do, the social significance of the Franciscans began to decline (102–4).

By mid-century the lax friars were bringing severe criticism to the order, and Scudder's rich knowledge of the literature of the period showed the low regard that even ordinary people had for the friars. Bonaventura's accession as Minister-General marked a new beginning, so much so that he is often considered the second founder. Over the years Scudder had steeped herself in the work of the major writers of the order as well as in the literary critics of these men. She made every effort to show the spiritual impetus of the moderates as well as of the spirituals and to clarify their concern for and their vision of the role of the order in the Church. Bonaventura emerged as a much stronger, more admirable figure here than in *Brother John*. Certainly Scudder herself could identify more with him than with Francis, although there is never any indication here that Bonaventura was bothered with doubts as to the legitimacy of his role or the conformity of his life with the rule he professed, as Scudder had so often been in her life.

As Minister-General, Bonaventura addressed himself immediately to the external and internal criticisms of the order. He defended the order in several famous debates, and Scudder presented

the arguments on both sides. Francis's rejection of corporate possessions had challenged medieval society, and Scudder sensed the
puzzlement of Bonaventura (as well as other confused Christians),
unable to reject or defend, yet not quite clear either about how to
live the divine paradox that had inspired Francis's life (177–82).
Nevertheless, she blamed the heroes of the order, like Bonaventura,
great though their contributions, for denaturing the ideal of Francis.
Thanks to them the order had become one of the great institutions
of society rather than a challenge to the social order (183–84).
Indeed it was Bonaventura's attempt to legitimize practices already
existing in the order that led to the distinction between *Usus* and
*Dominium*, use and power. This technicality was clarified shortly
after Bonaventura's death in the papal bull, "Exiit Qui Seminat,"
making the Papacy the holder or trustee for the properties of the
Franciscans (198–204).

Despite papal bulls and directives from Ministers-General, there
were many who clung to Francis's Will. Scudder's sympathy for
these radicals or conservators of the Franciscan ideal is clear. The
suggestion that Francis's Will and Rule be handed over to those
who really felt that they could live by it underscored the fundamental disunity as well as the fear of division in the order. The
troubles of the "Poor Hermits" introduced a new question—authority. Francis insisted that the office, not the man, had the
authority, but Scudder found that the hermits were now not so
concerned with poverty as with maintaining their privileges—
specifically the privilege of choosing their own authority (209–34).
Between the death of Pope Clement in 1315 and the accession of
John XXII in 1316 many of the hermits had been burnt at the
stake, imprisoned, forced into exile, or into outward conformity.
Michael of Cesena, the new Minister-General, fearing the separa-
tist movement, attempted a "middle way" to eliminate grave abuses
and appealed to Pope John XXII to curb the zealots. As a result,
the Poor Hermits were suppressed in 1317. The spirit of radicalism
was silenced and unity preserved for a time. Had Pope John been
satisfied he would have avoided the most acrimonious debate of
all. But a few years later he reopened the question of the Poverty

of Christ so thoroughly discussed seventy-five years before. Strangely enough, his attempt, unlike the attempts of the Franciscan leaders, succeeded in uniting the whole order. Conservative and radical, lax and regular, rallied to the defense of what each in his own way saw as the core or heart of the teaching of Francis.

Pope John heard all the experts. Scudder noted his tactical coup in revoking the privileges given to friars in papal bulls by which ownership of their properties and endowments was placed in the hands of the Pope. The friars who had hidden behind the Papacy as trustee now stood revealed as great land holders and were forced to face the issue of poverty squarely. The following year the Pope condemned the decisions of his predecessors that acknowledged the Poverty of Christ and his Apostles, making all who held to this heretics. John's decision struck at both monk and friar and raised two questions that continue to puzzle the sincere Christian. What is the proper attitude of the Christian to private property? What is the duty of obedience to mistaken or unjust authority? These questions that were of such moment in the religious atmosphere of the medieval world were eventually transferred to the political and commercial sphere and, to Scudder, were at the heart of modern social ethics (247–61). Scudder's detailed history of the struggle ended with 1323. The spirituals were routed but the ideal persisted. Part II ends with the story of one of the *fraticelli* burnt at the stake for adhering to the doctrine of the Poverty of Christ, a somewhat unnecessary drawing out of the materials so carefully presented in the preceding chapters (263–79).

**Part III: The Life Within.**    As Scudder looked back over the first century of the Franciscan Order, the failure and success of the adventure seemed to be sides of one coin. Certainly the Franciscan attempts had not been successful. Yet the persistence of this ideal over the centuries testified to its truth. Why did it so consistently fail, then just as regularly reappear? Scudder suggested that people failed to look at the real obstacles in the way, the unjust social order which was threatened by such an ideal. Scudder was writing this history just as the capitalist system was on the brink of disaster, and the Franciscan experience offered a salutary lesson, the Christian response to the Russian experiment then in progress.

Scudder realized that this struggle recorded so faithfully was only one facet of the Franciscan story. Part III, "The Life Within," was essential to her study, for without that life within the very controversy would not have existed. Her brief survey of the Franciscan contribution to missionary work, to art, architecture, literature, and science showed how much the Franciscans meant to the world even in the thirteenth century.

Scudder singled out some of the great Franciscan writings for special study. All of these are by the spirituals, but, nevertheless, in these sections Scudder is at her best. The "Sacrum Commercium," an allegory of the mystical marriage of Saint Francis with Lady Poverty, written shortly after the death of Francis, "one of the most perfect prose poems bequeathed by the Middle Ages," is retold in her most charming style (303). Here was Franciscan reading of Christian history up to that time. Here was real Franciscan joy, even while the troubles detailed in her history were brewing. The concluding reply to the Lady by the two friars pointing to the world below—"This is our cloister, O Lady Poverty"—is a phrase that, in the light of the story and of Scudder's application of this to modern days, held a meaning even she dared not enlarge on (313).

Her commentary on Angelo Clareno's "Exposition of the Rule" showed the intellectual outlook of the spirituals and their practical approach to the ideal of Francis. Her analysis pointed out the fusion of the spiritual and the social here while admitting that Angelo, too, made no direct application of Francis's Will to the world at large (315–30). The famous "Lauds of Jacopone da Todi" is discussed to show the variety of experiences among the friars. Jacopone's most famous laud pictured Poverty as that progressive stripping of self necessary for entrance into the reality which is the "Naughting" or "Annichilitade" known to the intimates of Saint Francis. But Jacopone's "Lauds" are instructive, not for what they said of Poverty, but for what they showed of the freedom and love of God which was the end or goal of poverty.

To Scudder, the ideals of Francis were so deep in the subconscious of the race that they would continue to flash before men and women, and preserving that vision was the great achievement of the Franciscans. In keeping with her own evolutionary approach Scudder felt that this Franciscan ideal had to move beyond the purely personal to the social before it would be completely successful. Each chapter of Franciscan history helped this evolution (332–51).

Her last chapters, "The Franciscan Defeat," "The Franciscan Achievements," and "The Franciscan Promise," reviewed ideas that came through more clearly in Part II. Her thesis that the experiment failed was only half her story as these three successive attempts to conclude the book indicate. Truth cannot fail, and the modern seeker must learn from Francis that to unite the spiritual and social is not easy but necessary. Even the defeat of Francis was an achievement, too, if one learned from him the inadequacy of individual attempts to solve social problems. Franciscans encountered a world organized on principles by which they refused to live and they withdrew from that world. Once they became separatists or elitists they were doomed to defeat. Measure them by what they did, and their achievements stand beside or even above their contemporaries in all areas of life. All such measurements still miss the essential radiance, which is their lives, not their deeds. Francis's stress on the importance of life, his belief in a way of life leading to God by loving fellowship with creatures, is the story of a successful adventure. But it is the responsibility of each age to build on the achievements of its predecessors, and Scudder bade modern adventurers fuse the spiritual with the social and economic, for a new version of Franciscan joy for the world (354–402).

The book was widely and, on the whole, favorably received. No one could fault her scholarly research into medieval sources and her easy presentation. Negative criticism centered around the separation of the mystical or ascetical impulses from the social in Franciscanism and on the constant intrusion of her own socialist outlook or bias, especially where readers were able to draw their own moral. Roman Catholic reviewers had similar reservations. Two outstanding Catholic Franciscan scholars who knew Scudder well wrote lengthy reviews—Father Cuthbert, O.S.F.C., of Assisi, for the *Tablet* (London) and Father Dunstan, O.S.F.C., of Providence, R. I., for the *Catholic World*.[11] Still, there was such divergence of opinion among reviews in other Catholic journals that *Catholic Library World* requested a Franciscan, Reverend James Meyer, O.F.M., to review the book from his background as a Franciscan and as editor of the *Franciscan Herald* and *Third Order Forum*. He praised Scudder's scholarly approach and her genuine sympathy with the struggle she recounted. "At the same time," he wrote, "were the author's work limited strictly to detailing the progress of that struggle, she would leave us a truer book. It is when she undertakes to give the philosophy of the movement that she, like many another well-intentioned Franciscanist, falls short of the truth." Only one with a thorough knowledge of Catholic asceticism could handle "so exquisitely Catholic a thing as Francis and Franciscanism."[12] Sabatier's wish for a historian-philosopher-sociologist was yet to be fulfilled.

## Saint Francis and Today

Again intimacy with the saints directed Scudder into new fields of social concern. She had always been in close contact with the Church of England, and now she was anxious to transmit the social vigor of English Catholic thought to the church in America through the Summer Schools for Christian Social Ethics held on the Wellesley campus in the 1930s. Then in 1933 she organized, in cooperation with Professor Edwin Booth of Boston University, an Institute for Franciscan Studies held at Adelynrood in the summer. Outstanding scholars and church leaders were invited to attend. Though this was one of the most memorable of many conferences at Adelynrood, Scudder was disappointed that none of her Roman Catholic Franciscan friends attended. Church unity was increasingly important in her social outlook, and she felt there were official constraints behind the letters of regret.[13] For years her prayer for the reconciliation of classes had been twinned with prayer for the reunion of Christendom, and to Scudder this meant bridging the Reformation gap. While she found in the Anglican faith her personal quest for God, she was just as certain that building up the body of Christ meant reconciliation with Rome. The conference lectures and round-table discussions dealt with the general topic "St. Francis and Today," and the summary statements in the report indicate Scudder's influence in the formation and direction of the discussions, especially those touching areas of modern society that could be significantly changed by the application of the principles of St. Francis: poverty and property, work and reward, war and peace. These areas were of particular concern in the 1930s, and Scudder had been led by her Franciscan studies and the economic distress in the country to reconsider her ideas on property. Though not all, or even the majority, at the Institute were ready to go as far as she, they did recognize that unrestricted access to or right of private property were "causal in many present social ills" and that the Franciscan ideas of property for "use" and not for "power" were valid principles for social action.[14]

In a pamphlet, *The Christian Attitude toward Private Property*, written the following year for the series *New Tracts for New Times*, Scudder disagreed flatly with the teaching of the Roman Catholic Church that private property was an individual right and that property was an extension of personality. That teaching, she said, should lead the Roman Church to take sides with those socialists who agreed with them and therefore demand that property of the kind required for full development of personality be made accessible to all citizens. Scudder here addressed herself to the principle that most Christians used to defend private property, stewardship. But this principle had to be reexamined in light of new times, and in the modern industrial society the stewardship principle failed because it did not examine the source of wealth as well as the use of wealth.[15]

Even more dangerous because more deceitful was the power that wealth or property conveyed, which just as effectively limited personality, both for the rich and poor. Intuitively the Franciscans, she said, recognized the danger in wealth or property even for the good Christian steward when they worked out so clearly the distinction between property for use and property for power. Wisely, Francis denied to his intimates "the insidious joy of generosity, with its lure to complacent self-righteousness" (5–7).

What was Scudder's solution? A socialism that would not interfere with personal property but would eliminate private profit in industry and socialize all means of production. Again, she did not concern herself with details or the means by which such socialism could be introduced. More important to her was the effect of a socialized society on character, a point she had discussed in detail in *Socialism and Character* twenty years earlier.

To the argument, so obvious in that decade, that such a system could not be introduced without violence or maintained without coercion she offered the Power that inspired sacrificial passions and that was capable of producing that voluntary surrender which was true freedom. This awakening of the Christian social conscience was at the heart of Scudder's thought and the object of her work in the church in recent years. Scudder did not for a moment intend to infringe on personality but stressed the importance of full development of personality in all social systems. Personality was not only "independent of possessions but incompatible with them," as outstanding leaders had shown in their own lives (12–13).

In 1934 Scudder spoke on "Christian Citizenship" to a meeting of the Woman's Auxiliary to the National Council meeting in Atlantic City and recalled the distance that the Anglican Church had travelled in less than fifteen years. In 1920 the Lambeth Conference had rejected the plea of Bishop Gore that the church demand a change in the structure of the economic system. In 1933 a pastoral letter of the American bishops demanded a "new order in which there would be more equitable distribution of wealth." She applauded the church here because at least it seemed to have learned from its experience in the war and postwar years, and she hoped that the leaders would adhere to their role as "Church."[16]

She urged the women to socialize their inner life, to examine their role as consumers and educators and above all their attitudes toward war and peace (20–21).

Ecumenism, too, had come a long way in ten years, and Vida Scudder made no secret of her elation when in 1945 the editors of *Franciscan Studies*, a quarterly review under the auspices of the three major Franciscan branches in the Roman Catholic Church, asked her to review Ralph Huber's *A Documented History of the Franciscan Order, 1182–1517*. Huber's book also discussed divisions in the order, and the editors turned to her as one thoroughly acquainted with its history. That the Franciscans not only went outside the order but outside the Roman Catholic communion for this review was a special joy to her.[17] In her notice Scudder emphasized the basic unity, despite all the differences, in the friars' attempt to avoid ownership which still troubled them, according to Huber's study. Her review concluded as did her own book on Saint Francis and her later study of Anglican monasticism: "Yet the Franciscan Order endures. Its commitments are distinctive, its achievements astonishing. Who can fail to recognize in the constant 'concern' shown throughout its history, a prophetic leaven, a challenge to us all? ... May we not hope that it will have special help today to offer our stumbling and hesitant feet?" (99).

Scudder's age placed great restriction on her activity in the last decade of her life, but her mind was still keen. In 1945 she joined a group of churchmen in the second annual conference on Christian Social Teachings at the Episcopal Theological School in Cambridge, Massachusetts. The papers were edited by Joseph Fletcher as *Christianity and Property*. Scudder's essay, "Anglican Thought on Property," did not break new ground but was a careful, graceful review of the development of social thought in the Anglican Church from the days of the Reformation. But there was always a modern ring to Scudder even as she looked again at the danger of power or *Dominium* in stewardship. Her question "Is escape from the danger of power, disguised as benevolence, possible for millionaires—or for nations?" might well fit into the call of the 1980s for a liberation theology or for a new American response to the Third World (129). In dedicating the volume to Scudder her colleagues acknowledged more than her work toward a better society for all. As in the case of the Franciscans, her life meant more than her achievement. To each of them, to know her then was "to have a lively foretaste of the communion of saints."[18]

## Chapter Seven

# Lives Worth Living:
# *On Journey* and
# *Father Huntington*

*On Journey*

In 1932, buoyed up by the positive response to her *Franciscan Adventure* and still revelling in that privilege of age—retirement, Scudder began work on her autobiography. She was gradually moving into yet a third stage in her career, but still she wrote free from the daily pressure of classes, lectures, and meetings. Though very different in style and tone, *On Journey* and *The Franciscan Adventure* vindicated the criticisms of her colleagues and publisher that her literary work suffered from her over-involvement in social issues. For each is, in its own genre, good literature.

*On Journey* is remarkable for its great joie de vivre. Here are seventy-five years of social history, tumultuous years in the history of the United States, told by an active, though almost forgotten participant in so many facets of that story. The charm of the book is that Scudder obviously enjoyed looking back over those years as much as she did living through them. The gaiety she mentioned so often in her Franciscan studies is very evident here. Most of the radical causes for which she worked neither survived nor succeeded, but that was not a concern; what mattered most was "infinite desire." She confessed to feeling "bitter" at times over these defeats, but for one who could still taste the pickles at those Brotherhood suppers and was even at that writing a dominating figure in Reinhold Niebuhr's Fellowship of Socialist Christians, "bitter" was hardly the word.

The preamble, written in 1932 from the Uffizi Gallery in Florence, is the most solemn part of the book. As she gazed on the pageantry of life presented in the religious art around her, her mind darted back to the murals on the walls of the New School of Social Research in New York and the modern pageant including the stock exchange and the New York subway—what she described as the rout of the capitalist order. In her mind's eye the murals blurred and became one great design as the religious and the secular so often did for her. To show the relation between the sacred and the secular in art, in literature, and in social theory had been at the heart of all her work. Such brief moments of revelation made Scudder feel sure of her path.

*On Journey* is a delightful autobiography. One is tempted to compare it to this or that in her other books, but it is so much more than the sum of all the others, just as the life of Scudder to those who have looked at it at all is so much more than the sum of all its parts. *On Journey* is not a historical account of her life and times, although it is the only account there is, but a story much like her life. In the manuscripts (there are six handwritten copybooks at Smith College), at first meditations or reflections that then became the draft of *On Journey,* she comments, a bit regretfully perhaps, that she never achieved any great renown, never assumed the leadership in any of the causes she initiated or served.[1] In chapter after chapter of *On Journey* the focus is seldom on herself. Rather than dominating the stage she is in the background, supplying ideas or cue lines and examining again the forces or impulses moving her in one direction and then another.

In an earlier essay, "The Privilege of Age," Scudder admitted that she enjoyed being old much more than she did being young.[2] *On Journey* implies the same. The vividness with which she recreated, almost relived, the unreality of her childhood is matched by the intensity of the young college girl, the exuberance of the Christian Socialist, the indignation of the reformer, and the enthusiasm of the college teacher. In all these accounts *On Journey* has a lightness, a sureness of touch, a complete lack of self-consciousness, and a quiet humor that captivates the reader. Scudder has a refined sensitivity that permits her to speak intimately about her personal life without sentimentalizing and with just enough reticence about her interior life to be convincing and sincere. Few have written so frankly and beautifully of the importance of female friendship or shown it in their lives.

*On Journey* is the best introduction to Scudder, and a bit of a relief to reread after some of her earlier writing. Here she discarded proselytizing and tried simply to explain her own role. *On Journey* is never awkward or contrived, polemical or repetitious. It does make the critic wonder whether literature might have gained had she followed a different path. Clearly, the books written in these years, *The Franciscan Adventure, Brother John, On Journey,* are much better as literature. But *On Journey* also makes one realize why Scudder was such a force in her own day and why she is today remembered for her role in so many different areas. It is easy to see her here as teacher, lecturer, group animator, and loving friend. *On Journey* makes it clear that it was the person of Scudder more than her ideas that inspired and challenged.

In this autobiography Scudder referred frequently to the *Bhagavad-Gita,* the oriental classic, precious legacy from her father. As she approached her eightieth year she was prepared to accept stillness at last and put aside "all loves born of purpose" (434). Hardly had she penned the words when she was asked to write a biography of Father Huntington, founder of the Order of the Holy Cross and of the monastic tradition in the Episcopal Church in America.

### Father Huntington: Founder of the Order of the Holy Cross

Shortly after the death of Father James O. S. Huntington, O.H.C., in 1935, Father Allen Whittemore, then Superior of the Order of the Holy Cross, approached Vida Scudder to write the biography of the founder.[3] For Scudder, it was a distinct privilege, for her friendship with Huntington went back to the early days of her own career, and it was a compliment to her literary ability as well. To write a biography of a contemporary has many pitfalls, and Scudder's work caused considerable controversy within the order. Some questioned her interpretation of Huntington's vision for the society. Others felt she had used Huntington as a foil for her own views.[4] She certainly saw this as an opportunity to show how a modern Christian reconciled the ideal and the real.

Scudder divided Huntington's life neatly into three sections— his childhood and youth, the early days as priest and monk in New York City, and the later years in Maryland and West Park, New York. She had access to memoirs and personal reminiscences of Huntington's family and religious associates, and she created an almost idyllic picture of his youth in New England and New York. The completely integrated personality Scudder admired so in later years she traced to a childhood in a New England family of means and culture and to the family's high religious and social convictions. She was almost envious of the loving, easy relationship among the brothers, sisters, and parents. That James followed his father and brother to the ministry was not surprising. Nor, considering the move his father, Frederick Dan Huntington, then Bishop of Central New York, had made from Unitarianism to the Episcopal Church, was it a shock to the family when James revealed a special call to the monastic life. Monasticism was still strange and suspect to the Episcopal Church in America, but the way had been paved by the Church of England. Scudder adroitly passed over the difficulties of the Society of St. John the Evangelist (Cowley Fathers) in the United States and kept the focus on Huntington rather than on modern monasticism.

Shortly after James Huntington had advanced to the priesthood, his call to found a monastic community completely attuned to the peculiar needs of America crystallized, and with two like-minded young ministers, he began a novitiate in 1881 in a house in the lower east side of New York City. They worked in connection with a mission started by the Sisters of Saint John the Baptist

(Cleever Sisters) and in their house conformed to the monastic Hours and traditions. Huntington's two companions did not continue in the society, and in 1884 he took public vows as the sole member of the community he had founded. Although the event caused a great stir in the church, Bishop Henry C. Potter, then Co-adjutor Bishop of New York, and James's father, Bishop Frederick Dan Huntington, appreciated the need for this spiritual supplement to the parish ministries and were prepared for such criticism. For twelve years Huntington worked among the poor in New York City, in the forefront of the pioneering efforts of that church in social reform, championing the labor movement, the eight-hour day, tenement house reform, child labor laws, and a consumers' league. Scudder knew him in these days as a crusader for social justice but claimed he was "in sad need of some constructive vision" (134). He eventually found this in Henry George's Single Tax which he felt provided the fundamental reconstruction necessary for industrial America.

Scudder painted a lively picture of Huntington, Father McGlynn, and Henry George in the political and economic upheavals in New York City, and at the same time noted Huntington's misgivings about the infringements of the political on his religious life.[5] Two other men had joined him in the order, but by 1892 Father Huntington realized that the tradition he felt called to establish in the church would not flower in the hurly-burly of the tenement district. The small group moved first to a house in New York City, then to Westminster in Maryland, and eventually to its permanent monastery in West Park, New York. Scudder's interpretation of Huntington's reason for moving was at the heart of the major criticisms of the book. She implied that his vision of an order that would combine the monastic life with active work for the oppressed was not shared by his colleagues, and this led him to realize that he was trying to climb two mountains at once without first laying firm foundations.

Almost half the book is given to a study of Huntington's life and work after he left New York City to concentrate chiefly on the development of the young order. At Westminster, Huntington drew up the rule for the order, basically Augustinian, combining active work in parishes far beyond the confines of the monastery with a monastic life centered around the liturgical Hours, the Opus Dei, and enjoining on members the vows of poverty, chastity, and obedience.

Scudder paid particular attention to the vows as taken in this order, especially the vow of poverty, which was of special interest to her own revolutionary Franciscan world view. That Huntington tied this to good works rather than to mortification, to a Franciscan social compunction rather than to a monastic asceticism, gave the rule a modern outlook and was another indication of that evolving social conscience she prayed for. Yet this contemporary attempt to live a life of evangelical poverty pointed out even more clearly the unreality of such a life, which was the essential problem of her beloved Franciscans. However, Father Huntington understood these problems even when he drew up the rule. Scudder noted his response to one of his boys in New York City who told him of his desire to enter the priesthood: "You will understand that I have lived among the poor; I know how they eat, how they work; I know how they live, starve, suffer. But I will never know how they feel, how they think. You know that" (211). Despite this experience, Huntington had no hesitation in enjoining poverty on members of the order, for he recognized that the counsel pointed inward and concerned the members' relationship to one another and their personal desire for closer union with God (214–15). Scudder, of course, longed to see a broader application of this principle to society.

In discussing the vow of obedience, Scudder seemed to be influenced more by contemporary events than by her knowledge of medieval history. Her understanding of the great religious orders of that period should have given her a clearer insight into the charism of the founders of each new society and the sense and manner in which each order lived its commitment. No wonder Father Whittemore, in his preface to the book, took exception to her connection of obedience and authority with the totalitarianism rampant in the 1930s, (10–11, 296–99), to what Ellen Gates

Starr earlier had called her essential Protestantism.[6] Scudder admitted that Huntington well knew the evangelical counsels were
not meant for the majority although they did "point the way to
the lines along which all should move." Nevertheless, Scudder saw
the prophetic element in such orders as more important. To her,
"the spiritual attitude which the Father Founder so rightly stressed
as primary, must not only in a religious order but in all Christian
groups demand its outward, sacramental expression" (226). Scudder confessed that Huntington would never see this as justifying
the reasons for a religious order. Still, such comments showed the
fundamental differences between Scudder and Huntington and explain why so many felt she used Huntington as a foil.

Scudder, however, would not agree with historians such as
Henry May in *Protestant Churches and Industrial America* (1949)
or Paul Carter in *The Decline and Revival of the Social Gospel*
(1956) that Huntington abandoned the cause of social justice for
mysticism or monasticism.[7] Her own long association with Huntington as preacher and director of retreats assured her that he had
never abandoned his concern for social justice although he certainly redirected it.[8] His convictions on those issues remained
firm, but as primary leader of this religious group he had to sacrifice openly espousing causes that might be politically controversial.
This surrender of the will, obedience to the higher will of the
group, or, as her Franciscans would say, "Naughting," demanded
greater courage and greater sacrifice. However, Scudder found
Huntington's social thought dated, distinctly pre-World War I
(284). He might be concerned over the vexing question of endowments for his order, but the fundamental question to Scudder
still was the source of the wealth, how that money had been made.
Questions that took on new dimensions in the twentieth century—
war, peace, pacifism, communism, trade unionism—did not concern
him (282–84). Nor would the focal point of his intercessory
prayer be the reconciliation of classes and the reunion of Christendom as it had been for Scudder for many years.

Many critics objected to Scudder's emphasis on the social concerns of Father Huntington, but this comment must have come

chiefly from those who had known Huntington as the serene pastor of souls rather than the fiery reformer. Scudder knew him in both roles and for this reason saw a greater continuity in his life than did others. Huntington was a radical Christian in Scudder's estimation, not because of his social views but because he had gone to the root of the Christian message. Scudder went further than Huntington in applying these Christian tenets to society and in this sense was still more radical or revolutionary. Because Henry May's study focused on the years prior to 1900, he referred to Scudder as Huntington's "far less radical disciple." There is little to indicate in this biography or in any of Scudder's writings that she was in any sense a disciple of Huntington.[9] Both were committed Christians who followed different paths to the same goal. Huntington's was not so radical, but he followed it without hesitation. Scudder was always the "beyond woman," ever looking for new paths to the Kingdom of justice on earth.

Was her picture of Huntington over-kind? Her only major criticism of James Huntington was his lack of radical social vision. However, James Arthur Muller's review article in the *Historical Magazine of the Protestant Episcopal Church* the following year raised a few questions about her objectivity.[10] Scudder was vague herself when she spoke of Huntington's evasiveness and inconsistency (141). Certainly the letter of Bishop Potter to which Scudder and Muller referred was not evasive. On issues raised in the letter, the irrevocability of the vows and the social orientation of the order, Scudder had made her own observations, but Huntington obviously preferred not to enter the debate on either issue and Scudder made no comment on this (96–102). In other instances, too, the historian might expect to find better documentation, but overall this is a biographical study that fully integrates all facets of Father James Huntington's life and presents a well-balanced portrait of a much-loved contemporary.[11]

## Chapter Eight

# Of Pacifism, Feminism, and Friendship

In 1939 Scudder published a selection of her essays entitled *The Privilege of Age: Essays Spiritual and Secular*, which had appeared earlier in a variety of journals and magazines. These essays ranging from "Plato as a Novelist," "Christian Conflicts," "Thanksgiving in Hard Times," to "A Little Tour in the Mind of Lenin" are an indication of the breadth of her interests.[1] She continued to be in the storm center of advanced thought in the church and in society, supporting by her name and by her writing such groups as Reinhold Niebuhr's Fellowship of Socialist Christians and Rufus Jones's Wider Quaker Fellowship. She worked closely with the Christendom group in England, encouraged Mother Pattie Ellis in her desire to establish the Community of the Way of the Cross, a women's religious order combining active social work with monastic life, and followed closely the Reverend Frederick Hastings Smyth's Society of the Catholic Commonwealth.[2] No one could ever call Scudder outdated. Her socialist position continued to evolve, and while it is impossible here to examine her views on every social issue, it is important to look at two that have taken on renewed importance in the last half of this century: pacifism and feminism.

### Pacifism

Scudder's position as an absolute pacifist withstood the acid test of World War II and the Cold War. A review of her journey to pacifism, a more difficult one for her than her path to socialism, is an example of the gradual evolution of social thought she spoke of so often. Her early conversion to Christian Socialism was an intellectual one, supplemented and modified by her experiences in the settlements and in the labor movement. At first her socialism appealed to the privileged to bridge the gap between the classes, and it was in this hope that she initiated the College Settlements Association. Then, in the labor strife of the 1890s, she became aware of the real meaning of the class struggle and gradually accepted the violence implicit in this struggle.

In Scudder's published writing at this time there is little reference to the question of war or peace, or to international relations at all. The first glimpse of any serious reflection on war and peace is in a long personal letter to her friend Ann Whitney in 1904. Here she looked back over the early years of her career and the blow that the Spanish-American War and the political events ensuing had given her. For more than a decade she had been active in reform movements in the country and she rejoiced in the steady advance of social thought she observed in America. Then suddenly she saw the United States "deliberately, serenely, uttering moral platitudes the while" moving back into the barbaric ages. "The whole spiritual surroundings of my life seemed to vanish and my aims and efforts ceased to have any point or any relation to the march of events." In this letter she disagreed with her friend's anti-imperialist stand because she felt the United States must now accept the responsibility for its sin. However, Scudder did not dwell on the situation in the Phillipines because that "crime has become to me only one symptom among others of the rottenness of our civilization, and no worse than others."[3] The war had at least made many Americans face up to the hollowness of their boasts. But there was no mention of peace as a moral imperative. To her, war and the industrial strife in the country were inseparable and led her to a more radical socialism, whereas colleagues like Helena S. Dudley and Jane Addams were moved to support peace movements.

Of course she believed war should be eliminated, but for the present the by-products of war, the subordination of the individual and a self-sacrificing leadership, not to mention the emotional

thrill that deeds of heroism evoked, had positive contributions for
an evolving socialist mentality. She saw a similar limited value in
trade unions where groups struggled together for a noble end.
Though she criticized the narrow vision of the unions, they, too,
were developing qualities necessary for the socialist state. But in
the final stages of the socialist revolution she did not rule out
violence. These ideas were spelled out in detail in her *Socialism
and Character*, but World War I was the testing ground for such
views. The years 1914–1917 gave American radicals and reformers
opportunity to reexamine their position, and Scudder's writings during these years indicate her ambivalence.

At a Church Congress in Virginia in 1916 Scudder urged religious leaders at least to give their sanction to the social ethic growing in the country. Although she did not deal directly with the
war issue in her main talk, "The Alleged Failure of the Church
to Meet the Social Emergency," Scudder replied very emphatically
to other speakers who did. She was puzzled by the argument that
self-defense was the "ultimate righteousness," but even more dismayed and troubled that nothing in the talks of previous speakers
went beyond the natural level of morality. Replying directly to a
paper on "Christianity in International Relations" which concluded
that there was no defense of pacificism in Christ's teaching, she
referred to herself not as a professed pacifist but as a spirit "on
journey." She found no express statements in Christ's message for
or against war either, but she did find in the life of Christ the
only chance for peace. Unless some nation was willing to offer
itself as a martyr and "break the vicious circle of the piling up of
armaments," peace would never come. The philosophy of preparedness was to her "a philosophy of fear."[4]

A few months later in "The Doubting Pacifist" (discussed in
Chapter 5), she gave a carefully considered view of war and pacifism. By this time the United States had entered the war and the
lines were more tightly drawn. She began with reference to the
oriental classic, *The Bhagavad-Gita.* To Arjuna who cannot bear
to kill his brothers, the charioteer, in reality the god Krishna, says,
in effect: "Don't worry you cannot kill them however hard you

try" (741–42). Scudder found a lesson here for the modern materialistic pacifist who thought man was final arbiter of human destiny. To denounce war for its willful destruction of personality and to show so little concern for the degrading and depersonalized conditions under which people lived was incongruous. No true pacifist should view war in isolation. "So long as conflicting interests are the ruling principle of the economic order," she wrote, the world would never "escape the curse of war" (742, 750–51).

Scudder had another reason for not joining the pacifist ranks. Her socialist principles at this time accepted the doctrine of the class struggle as a necessary weapon or tool in overturning the unjust economic system. She did not equate the class struggle with class warfare, but violence might be necessary at some stage in this socialist evolution. For this reason she felt the idealism of the pacifist in 1917 was premature but, nevertheless, an ideal to be respected and protected.

Scudder supported President Wilson's call for a League of Nations and hoped the countries emerging from the socialist revolutions in Europe would be admitted. She supported disarmament and the World Court and thus was thoroughly disappointed at the role of the United States in the immediate postwar years. Accurately sensing the mood of the country, she moved quickly to try to preserve the few advances in the churches in the previous decade and set in motion meetings that resulted in the Church League for Industrial Democracy. It was at this time that she met Norman Thomas and A. J. Muste, both committed to socialism and pacifism. When, in 1923, the Fellowship of Reconciliation recognized that peace could not be achieved in isolation and adopted a socialist position, Scudder joined, but her focus in that decade was still socialism. She was excited by the events in Russia and hoped the revolutions in Europe were a first stage in that industrial democracy she wrote of. As the decade moved along, she relinquished her Marxian concepts, realizing that a revolution imposed forcibly on people would never be successful. Now, instead of looking at the proletariat as the messianic unit, she turned to her historical study of the Franciscans and concluded that the best hope for advancing the classless society was in the minority groups that had always been the prophetic element in Christianity. These had always intrigued Scudder because in a variety of ways they exemplified the Christian Socialist mind-set of the future.

Scudder's autobiography is the best account of her mental and spiritual life in the 1930s. She wrote frequently during these depression years for such magazines as the *World Tomorrow*, the *Christian Century,* and *Radical Religion,* but in none of these does she discuss in detail her view on the ideological or political tensions in pacifist ranks. She herself, however, became stronger in her views on pacifism. Like many of her colleagues she no longer saw the class conflict as an issue in the United States. It was time for a new Christian-Marxist dialogue, and she tried to stimulate such a dialogue by keeping in touch with the Russian experiment though she found its methods more abhorrent than its professed atheism.[5] As the international situation worsened, Scudder maintained her pacifist stand, opposing the principle of collective security but at least willing to support a United Front. Better to join with the Communists, for, however harsh the means they used, at least they sought some release from unjust economic conditions. In such ways the Christian dialectic, she wrote, was "slowly, painfully, working out a synthesis of personal non-resistance with adherence to militant groups." But she realized that "martyrdom may lie along this road."[6]

Again, the years 1939–1941 gave pacifists in the United States time to readjust their thinking to the political reality. Scudder's only lengthy statement of her position is in "Foemen Vassals," which appeared in the *Protestant* just before Pearl Harbor. She deplored wrong methods and openly pointed to an anti-Semitism at the root of some pacifist thought. She was a pacifist not because she saw no difference between the two sides but because she refused to adopt the methods of the side she abjured.[7] Writing now as an absolute pacifist, she admitted that she could not even countenance the "potential violence" of a proletarian revolution. She regretted the fact that so many of the peace prophets were deserting the ranks, but she was just as concerned now as she was in 1917 that

Christians recognize that opposing convictions were also legitimate. She urged pacifists in wartime to seek out active work, work taxing to their mental or physical powers, and to recognize and accept the fact that even the soldier's role may be more valuable at the moment than the role of one who anticipated "the ethic of an unrealized, perhaps unrealizable future" (49–53). Almost prophetically she warned that it might be only the wisdom of science that would force nations to abandon war. Still, pacifism offered a higher motive and Scudder urged all pacifists to remember that they "must stand with the prophets." As children of that "future age" spoken of in the early Church they must remain firm in their conviction that "the possibility of extending the Christian law in its fullness to group action, is the most important matter that religion will be called on to face during the coming years" (53).

Although World War II was an extremely patriotic war, pacifists benefitted from the debates of the past twenty years. The conduct of the Axis powers had posed a real dilemma for pacifists of all persuasions in the 1930s, but the country had become more tolerant of the position of the conscientious objector and pacifist. Though most of Scudder's colleagues of early days had died by this time, her old friend Emily Balch, who suffered so for her pacifist views in 1917 and was awarded the Nobel Peace prize in 1936, came out in favor of war against Hitler while Scudder remained a pacifist. However, she followed her own advice and, once war was declared, did not continue open protest. The experience of the previous two decades had not only confirmed Scudder's pacifism, it also had refined her socialism. Writing in *My Quest for Reality* (1952), a sequel to her *On Journey*, she continued to show the unity she found in the secular and spiritual world. At ninety her mind and pen were still active, and she probed the whole question of disarmament in an atomic age. The Cold War had forced her to a new stage in her own socialist thought. "The primary call" coming from the Holy Spirit was for the "abolition of war," and this had taken precedence with her "over demands for economic reform, or any other plans for social welfare." She was glad to see the whole question of peace and disarmament entering the political arena. To Scudder, this was the new call of the prophets to clear the way for "the gradual establishment of the Kingdom of God on earth." Scudder herself was now ready to go further and "abandon even self-protection."[8]

## Feminism

Vida Scudder came to maturity in an age that revered family life and exalted the position of women as no previous age had. Yet at the close of the Victorian age many women strained against the confines of the roles assigned to them. In the United States a variety of social forces and reform movements called women out of the home, while "the cult of true womanhood," as one historian described it, still tried to hold back the times.[9] The organized movement for women's rights emerged at mid-century and encompassed a broad scope before focusing on the suffrage after the Civil War. By 1869 the struggle over suffrage had divided the movement into the National Woman Suffrage Association, led by Elizabeth Cady Stanton and Susan B. Anthony, and the more conservative American Woman Suffrage Association, led by the proper Bostonians, Lucy Stone Blackwell and Julia Ward Howe. By the time the two groups had united in 1890 as the National American Woman Suffrage Association, the suffrage issue had made little progress, but women had made substantial gains in other areas, particularly in higher education. Women's right to and success in higher education was an accepted fact, but how they should or could use this education was not quite so clear.

Vida Scudder was faced with this dilemma, and the severe physical and emotional illnesses at crucial moments of decision in her own life were a result of social rather than family pressures. In her sheltered youth Scudder had enjoyed the support of loving, interested, and socially concerned relatives. Her greatest struggle was with her own natural shyness. Yet she must have been aware of the restriction of opportunity for intelligent girls, for in her autobiography she recalled a secret dream of enrolling at Harvard disguised as a boy. Just as far-fetched was the hope which she dared not mention that her mother would send her to one of the new women's colleges. Fortunately Harriet Scudder was encouraged by her sister, Julia Dutton, then planning to study medicine, and her sister-in-law, Jeanie Scudder, an artist, to make the sacrifice that Vida's four years at Smith would entail.[10]

Scudder's background was then quite different from the pioneer feminists' and different, too, from that of many of her classmates at Smith. At Smith the emphasis was on the privilege and responsibility of the college woman in shaping society rather than on preparation for a competitive life in that society. It was while at Oxford that Ruskin's lectures alerted Scudder to her personal responsibility to the poor and to society as a whole. How to respond was not so clear in the Boston of 1885. A combination of influences, discussed in Chapter 1, led her to teaching, to settlement work, and to socialism. Although she never felt personally, in her chosen careers, the discrimination or lack of opportunities other women did, Scudder became increasingly aware of the fact that women suffered most from the injustices of a capitalist society. Most of her life was spent in work with and for women, opening new horizons for women in all walks of life. Over the years Scudder's primary and deepest relationships were with women, and any study of Scudder must consider the impact of her work, her writing, and her life on women.

In 1887, while still groping for her own role, Scudder contributed to the *Christian Union* a series of articles reflecting on the effect of higher education on character. Higher education for women, she felt, was one of the most far-reaching reforms of the past half-century and, contrary to current arguments, gave the young woman a better approach to home duties. The discontent so marked among middle-class women was not characteristic of the college woman who now saw marriage as a deliberate choice, not as the only alternative. However, the day was not far off when the educated woman would carry her role of homemaker to the social sphere and concern herself with the housing of the poor, public morality, and the wages of women. Unless women were aware of such issues and of their power to influence them, of what use was the ballot? Scudder criticized the suffragists whose bazaars displayed women's petty pastimes beneath banners proclaiming "Our powers demand our rights." Scudder saw suffrage as a duty, not a right, and while she believed it should and would come, women must be prepared to perform this duty wisely. Impatient with the religious and ethnic prejudices in the suffrage debate in Massachusetts, she warned women that if they used the ballot simply to protect their own private interests, it would do little to change society or the status of women in society.[11] For this reason Scudder herself was never involved directly in the suffrage movement although she supported it. It was far more important to society that women become aware of the inequities of the economic system.

Scudder questioned many of the basic assumptions about the nature of women, but in her early essays there is some ambivalence. She was gradually divesting herself of ideas about true womanhood but still tended to view women as upholding the ideal and the ethical, and men as urging the practical and the expedient.

In 1889 she wrote a lengthy essay in *Poet Lore*, "Womanhood and Modern Poetry," contrasting particularly the poetry of Shakespeare and Browning. Both poets praised women more for their virtue and intelligence than for merely physical beauty, but Browning went further. His women were more often the protagonists; the poet's understanding of woman's nature explained the essential quality of the roles he assigned to them. Shakespeare's women were absolutely good or abnormally evil and therefore more simple in nature than men. Browning had women take part in all the activities of men because they had no particular goodness or simplicity to set them apart. In this Browning had even gone beyond his age, had taken woman down from her pedestal and placed her in the world in which most women lived. But Browning saw women as more "sensitive, more intricately framed." Did Scudder see this as a step backwards, trading sensitivity for intellectual equality? No, both Shakespeare and Browning stressed moral preeminence, but Browning, she felt, had grasped the reality of the nineteenth century, the reality "beneath all the agitation, absurdity and talk, that it is in the world, not without it, that women are henceforth to live."[12]

Scudder herself had doubts about woman's moral superiority, about the distinctively womanly character. Sympathy, tenderness, high spiritual ideals, if they ever were woman's, she told the Association of College Alumnae, were enhanced by education to include greater executive power, broader interests, and deeper understanding. The world had need of this combination of powers. Although most of this audience would not agree with her that the entire society needed reconstruction, Scudder used opportunities such as this to interest college women in the new settlement work, for she was convinced that once intelligent women were involved in social reforms, they would realize the system was unjust at the core. The ballot itself would not change the system.[13]

Increasingly, Scudder's view on the status and role of women showed her growing socialist commitment. She opened an article on "Woman and Socialism" in the *Yale Review* with the hope that the "habit of talking about Woman with a capital, as if she were an abstraction apart from humanity at large, will seem curiously old-fashioned sometime."[14] In this article, as in all her writing, Scudder took a positive, practical approach and concentrated not on the benefits socialism would bring to women, but on the contribution women could readily bring to the preparation for a new social system. For years women had done more than their share in producing, consuming, and distributing without any incentive of profit—admirable training for a socialist state. The usually genteel Scudder was thoroughly modern in her remark that women "really ought to turn when accused of not being practical" (461). Group consciousness, too, was far more evolved among women, and the nurturing, protective roles assigned them in the home were essential to a future-oriented state. Women, once they recognized the benefits of the socialist state, would need little retraining. These outward-directed qualities essential for men and women in a socialist society were discussed fully in her *Socialism and Character.*

Shortly after World War I broke out in Europe, Scudder looked at the impact of this crisis on the reform movements. In "Women and the Present Crisis" she claimed that the Woman Movement would be severely affected since the war undercut its basic assumption that militarism was outmoded and that the future of civilization depended on "a comity of nations." But the horrors of the war had caused all people to question such militarism and those theories of physical might which had so often been used to justify the exclusion of women from politics. Scudder carried that argument a step further and asked whether "a state governed in part by women would ever maintain the vast armaments which were sure sooner or later to be put to use?" But she did not simply counterbalance feminine sensitivity and masculine brutality. "Women are not one whit better than men," she wrote, but socialized down the ages to "the exercise of co-operative instincts" they were the "surest champions of international friendliness and peace."[15] Fifty years later a new wave of feminism reiterated this call for nothing less than human liberation on a world wide scale, and universal military disarmament.

If there is some uncertainty about the character and role of women in Scudder's early essays, written at a time when women's roles were discussed on all sides, there is no doubt about her views of women in her early novels. Neither *A Listener in Babel* nor *The Disciple of a Saint* was written as feminist literature, although *A Listener in Babel* was certainly a novel of protest. Both indicated very clearly her perception of women and women's roles. In *A Listener in Babel* Hilda Lathrop is "the new woman," educated, talented, dedicated, independent. Financially secure, Hilda lets neither family ties nor worldly ambition overcome the gnawing desire to find a meaningful life. In this book most of the women are stronger and have greater insight than the men. The heated discussions and easy interaction of both men and women show the natural relationship that should exist between the sexes. Romance is thinly interwoven into the story but is neither absolute nor all-engrossing. Scudder's style was not to denounce institutions long entrenched in society but calmly to suggest alternatives. Hilda's love for Dorothy was greater than her love for Lawrence Ferguson, as she had proven at least to herself. The ideal marriage of Dorothy to Hilda's own "beyond man" revealed the marital problem of many intelligent women. Dorothy admitted a real loneliness though she lived for her husband and children. Lawrence's love for his family enabled him to live beyond them for others, but Dorothy was not expected to share this part of her husband's life. Hilda measured her life against Dorothy's. She realized now that "fellowship in desire" was more important for some than the physical bond. As she talked with Dorothy, she recalled the days she had spent in retreat among strangers united by common ideals as "worth any marriage kiss."[16] The intimacy of mind and heart that she shared with Mildred Ellis, her co-worker, with Mr. O'Hagan, the labor leader, and with Katie Donovan, from the neighborhood, provided the human support Hilda needed. Nor is there any patronizing element visible in Hilda's plan to live and work with Katie Donovan to discover how the creative arts can be fostered in certain industries; one of Scudder's hopes for the settlement experiment was that it would bridge the gap between the classes. Daily life in Langley House also showed alternative life-styles and wider opportunities for women of courage. Janet Frothingham planned to edit an anarchist newspaper, Mildred Ellis to develop the full Christian cooperative life with a group living and working in a poor neighborhood, and Hilda hoped to use her creative talent to humanize a modern industry. Although not explicitly stated, the implication was that marriage was not necessary for feminine fulfillment.

In *The Disciple of a Saint* the hero is Neri, but unquestionably Catherine and Catherine's presence dominate the book. Catherine is poor and unlettered, but rich in love and highly intelligent. The courage and compassion that directed her to the care of the sick also aroused her concern for the spiritual needs of the world, and Catherine moved as surely among the men at the papal court as she did among the poor in Siena. In this novel the romantic element is stronger, more complicated than in *A Listener in Babel*, but despite Neri's great love for his cousin Ilaria, marriage was not the answer to his spiritual restlessness. Seldom in Scudder's writings, even in her earlier short stories, did the hero or heroine live happily ever after in marriage.

Years later, in *On Journey*, Scudder frankly admitted that marriage often seemed "terribly impoverished for women." She did recognize that perhaps, humanly speaking, she had missed a precious experience in not having had any real sexual interests beyond a desperate desire when young to fall in love (212–13). But Scudder was always the intellectual, and she was drawn to and related to men first on this level, even in her younger years. As she grew older, Scudder attracted many intimates among men young and old, clergy and social activists, writers and reformers, as well as academics. Many of these spoke fondly of her and to her as Aunt Vida or Mother Vida, forms of address she delighted in and even urged on people. Those whom she inspired, provoked, and challenged loved her for herself and for her deep religious commitment as well as for the stimulation of her ideas. The more intimate among these shared with her the full meaning of her favorite quotation from William Morris: "Forsooth, brothers, fellowship is heaven and the lack of fellowship is hell."[17] Scudder never railed against men and in practice worked with men in socialist and church groups on the levels she indicated in her novels.

## Fellowship

"Fellowship" was an essential element in Scudder's hope of a reconstructed society, and fellowship and friendship were important to her own personal life as well. No one has written more beautifully of friendship, especially among women, than Scudder did, nor does any life testify more to the need for and benefits of such friendships.[18] After a childhood lived almost entirely with adults Vida Scudder relished the long hours spent in intimate discussions of religion and life with her classmates at Smith and years later recalled those first encounters with her peers as "a staggering and absorbing experience" (66). Although naturally shy, Scudder was an affectionate person if not a loving one. Her love, once given, was given wholeheartedly. Her Smith classmate, Clara French, claimed a place in her heart which fifty years later Scudder remembered tenderly. In the class prophecy at Smith in 1884 French described Vida Scudder as a famous writer secretly working on "a treatise which is to be called, 'Friendship the Science of Sciences and the Art of Arts.' "[19]

In "Influence and Independence," written with Sophia Kirk in 1890, Scudder criticized independence in friendship which feared "infringing upon each other's intellectual rights or feelings." The result was "that friendship, among women at least, is often dwarfed to a mere matter of practical service or personal affection, and deprived of much that is most precious in human intercourse, of the higher sympathy, the free give and take of mental effort or achievement."[20] Scudder soon resolved such tensions or inhibitions in her own relations, and her deepest friendships dated from the early years of her career and endured a lifetime. Throughout her autobiography she wrote intimately of her own close ties with Clara French, Florence Converse, Lucy Smith, and Helena Dudley. Love among women, she knew, was deep and therefore not always smooth. As friendship grew and deepened, it required constant adjusting, and even the closest friends developed at different paces at different times. Life must be lived on all levels, and so, for true love among women, there must be a meeting of mind and spirit as well as natural attractions.

Love, she wrote, must guard against being possessive, though the heart may often be greedy. There is a necessary solitude that love must respect, a solitude essential to personality. Enough fragments of Scudder's letters are available to indicate traces of this eagerness for intimacy with friends whom she cherished. Guided by her even greater social outreach many of these close friends also became members of The Society of the Companions of the Holy Cross. Scudder had joined the Society in 1889, shortly after the sudden death of Clara French had made her fearful of opening herself to new personal friendships, and this group provided both privacy and a needed spiritual balm and support. As the Society developed, largely under Scudder's influence, it became the group closest to her in its corporate living as well as in the deep spiritual relationship that developed among the Companions through mutual prayer and interaction. Over the years Scudder introduced to the Society many Christian women deeply committed to social reform in their active life but conscious of the need of the support of prayer in their work and equally concerned with their own spiritual development.[21]

Scudder's own faith had been nourished by Harriet Scudder and the love between mother and daughter went beyond the usual devotion. The two were seldom separated for any lengthy period and though the mother never shared her daughter's radicalism, she knew it was her daughter's need and love for her mother, more than simple duty, that kept the two together for almost sixty years. It was not until 1919 that Florence Converse and Mrs. Caroline Converse, who had been living in Wellesley since 1912, came to live with the Scudders. The two friends had often spoken of sharing a home together, but it was only after her mother began to fail mentally that Scudder introduced anyone else into the household. Vida Scudder may have needed support at this time. More likely, until then Harriet Scudder was so accustomed to the New England privacy of family that she was not ready to make the required adjustments or to share her daughter with others. Certainly the idea of a corporate life, which Vida Scudder advocated so freely on so many levels, would not have appealed to her mother's fastidious nature.

A few years after Harriet Scudder's death in 1920 Helena Dudley and Lucy Smith, longtime friends and colleagues of Scudder and members of the Society of the Companions of the Holy Cross, joined the household on Leighton Road. In anticipation Scudder wrote excitedly to Ellen Gates Starr that next year she was to have "a real Companion House" and urged Starr to come too.[22] This recalls Mildred Ellis's intention in *A Listener in Babel* one day to form a cooperative community (304–12).

This early novel *A Listener in Babel* may be more revealing of Scudder if seen as a response to Florence Converse's *Diana Victrix*. Even less is known about the early life of Converse than of

Scudder, and there is little or no reference to this book beyond the fact of publication in Converse materials at Wellesley. Converse had been a student of Scudder's at Wellesley. After graduation in 1893 Converse returned to her native New Orleans and in 1897 published this first novel which she dedicated to her mother. That year, 1897, she returned to Boston, lived at Denison House for five years and then in suburbs of Boston. Converse was associate editor of the *Churchman* and then from 1908 until 1930 assistant editor of the *Atlantic Monthly*. Converse and Scudder were colleagues in radical causes as well as companions down the years in the most intimate secrets of the heart. Converse's *Diana Victrix* spoke very frankly of the exclusive love of the heroines Sylvia and Enid and their decision to live with and for each other.[23]

At this time Scudder began work on *A Listener in Babel*, which first went to the publishers in 1900. Was it her personal answer to Florence Converse or an attempt to show other viable life-styles for women? The homosocial world Scudder described depended on "fellowship of desire" which was more important than the personal bond. While Scudder's novel also presumed real love among women it focused on communal support rather than exclusive relations and demanded a commitment to society and to Christian living. In 1900 Converse's next book *The Burden of Christopher* showed more of Scudder's socialist influence and is dedicated "To Vida D. Scudder—her Book."[24] Was it with deliberation that *A Listener in Babel* appeared in 1903 without any dedication and *The Disciple of a Saint* in 1907 dedicated to Lucy Smith?

In 1912 Scudder dedicated her *Socialism and Character* "To Florence Converse, Comrade and Companion," followed by a long dedicatory note explaining the purpose of the book which reflected "their common thought" (v, vi). On the flyleaf of Converse's copy of *Socialism and Character* Scudder inscribed a poem which described their personal relationship.

> Lo, here is fellowschipe;
> One fayth to holde
> One truth to speake,

> One wrong to wreke,
> One loving-cuppe to syppe,
>   And to dippe
> In one disshe faithfullich
> As lambkins of one folde.
> Either for other to suffre alle thing.
>   One song to sing
> In swete accord and maken melodye.
> Right so thou and I good-fellows be:
> Now God prosper thee and me.[25]

Twenty-five years later Scudder dedicated her autobiography "To Florence Converse, Comrade and Companion" and continued: "Twenty-five years ago, writing from the holy mountain of La Verna, I dedicated my book, *Socialism and Character* to you in these same words. A quarter of a century is a long time; each passing year has deepened our loyalty to the ideas in that book, and the meaning to us of those words."

In this autobiography Scudder admitted that only rarely did one find the exquisite joy of a friend who shared "both jokes and prayers," and she was grateful for such a friend in Florence Converse (223). That same year, 1937, Converse dedicated her *Collected Poems* "To Vida D. Scudder" followed by the poem quoted above. In her autobiography Scudder hoped that some day the world would have an "In Memoriam" or sonnet-cycle "by a woman, of a woman" celebrating the "spiritual and intellectual comradeship" between them (219–20). Perhaps she dreamed that Converse would be the poet of their love, but, eighty-three at the death of Scudder, Florence Converse's keen mind and poetic speech failed quickly thereafter. Their friendship had indeed been "a staff on which to lean" during their journey (228). But beyond the reciprocal relationship of these two friends is the broader struggle of talented women to shape their own lives. This had always been a concern of Scudder and in many ways her life is a stronger statement for feminine self-determination than is her writing.

## Chapter Nine

# Conclusion

Vida Dutton Scudder remains an elusive figure in American letters and in religious social history. So far, what we know of her has been gleaned largely from her own writing, and for those who have tried to make some appraisal of her life and work the character and personality of Vida Scudder and her impact on her time seem to be so much more than the written word reveals. In her later years Scudder always referred to herself as a revolutionary, and were she to assess her career today, it would doubtless be as a revolutionary Christian and churchwoman. Those who knew her intimately would agree that as a radical Christian Scudder directed all her efforts toward advancing that socialist revolution she prayed for. She realized that no revolution would succeed unless the people were prepared mentally to accept it. This study has focused on her major published work to show the influences that shaped her growing radicalism and the means she used to develop a similar Christian Socialist mentality in her largely middle-class readers.

Scudder does not emerge as a major literary figure, nor even a secondary one; nevertheless, it is through her writing that she has made her greatest contribution to the evolution of Christian Socialist thought in the United States. Her writing drew to her men and women who took up her challenge and, goaded and encouraged by her, often seemed to move beyond their mentor on the social frontier. Though Scudder was always in the vanguard of social thinking, her writing style—rhythmic, coherent, and correct— had the gentility of the Victorians, which, sometimes to her advantage, obscured the radicalism of her message.

Scudder would have loved to have been more active on the social frontier herself but recognized the limitations of her talents.

She had initiated the college settlements which were testing ground and training school for so many Christian leaders. But her natural reserve found the daily intercourse of the settlement impossible; two days stitching in a factory were more than her frail body could endure; picketing with the neighborhood women was little more than a gesture of solidarity. Such experiences, however, convinced her of the importance of her role as spokesperson for these movements to her own professional and privileged class who were unaware of or unconcerned about the injustices to which they were party. If the settlements were undone by success, no small credit is due to Vida Scudder who inspired countless young men and women to support the work in whatever way they could.

As teacher, Scudder never forgot the obligation and opportunity that was hers so to present the literature of the ages that her students would see in all great art a revelation of the human condition. As lecturer and writer, she spoke and wrote not to the poor but to the privileged and to the intellectual whom she constantly challenged and with whom she was ready to stand in penitence. Still, she did not demand heroic sacrifice but an honest appraisal of one's individual life. She was all too conscious of the security and intellectual delight of the world in which she moved, and if the interior suffering her position caused her was not evident, this only added to her discomfort and sense of guilt.

Scudder was a serious scholar and writer. Challenging and stimulating, she was not a seminal thinker, but her keen intellect was always quick to see how the new related to, clarified, or advanced the traditional Christian truth. Despite the radicalism of her religious thought, Scudder was an acknowledged leader in the church at a time when women were seldom seen in any role but handmaiden. For more years than she ever dreamed in 1897, she was the woman for her own time. As we learn more about Scudder's role in church and in society, she may emerge as a woman for all times as well.

# Notes and References

*Chapter One*

1. As quoted by Winifred Hulbert in "Seventy-five Years of Progress in Social Justice," a paper presented to the Society of the Companions of the Holy Cross at Adelynrood, South Byfield, Mass., August 26, 1959. In Archives of the Society in Adelynrood, Byfield, Mass. (hereafter SCHC Papers).

2. Vida Dutton Scudder, *On Journey* (New York, 1937), pp. 15–18. Also a personal letter from Dorothy Jealous Scudder, New York, September 9, 1972. She was christened Julia Davida but there were already two Aunt Julia's in this household. She was called Vida for Davida, feminine form for the name of her father. When she was confirmed, she dropped the Julia and assumed her mother's maiden name for a middle name and was thereafter Vida Dutton Scudder.

3. Horace E. Scudder, ed., *The Life and Letters of David Coit Scudder* (Boston: E. P. Dutton, 1864), p. 10. Charles Scudder had two sons in his first marriage, a son and a daughter in a second marriage, and these three sons in his marriage to Sarah Coit Scudder. All of these married except his daughter Jeanie, an artist. *On Journey,* pp. 40–41.

4. *On Journey,* pp. 18–41, 49–53, 176. Another uncle, Thomas Dutton, died while she was quite young. Most of the biographical material is taken from this autobiography.

5. *On Journey,* pp. 57–68, 217–28.

6. Since this is the first published book on Vida Scudder and her own papers have been destroyed, the major articles located are included in the bibliography in chronological order.

7. "Recollections of Ruskin," The Contributors' Club, the *Atlantic Monthly,* 85 (April, 1900):570. *On Journey,* pp. 78–96.

8. *On Journey,* pp. 109–112, 141–43. Vida Dutton Scudder to Louise Manning Hodgkins, Wednesday, December 27, 1889, in Wellesley College Archives (hereafter WCA).

9. "The Place of the College Settlements," *Andover Review* 18 (October, 1892):334–45.

10. *On Journey*, pp. 155–57, 179–80. "Journal III," 1934–35, July 23, p. 23. There are six of these handwritten notebooks in Scudder papers in the Sophia Smith Collection, Smith College (hereafter SSC). At first they seem to be personal religious reflections but then become a draft of her autobiography.

11. Henry F. May, *Protestant Churches and Industrial America* (1949; rpt. New York, 1963), p. 242. H. H. Quint, *The Forging of American Socialism* (New York, 1953), pp. 112–17. C. H. Hopkins, *The Rise of the Social Gospel in American Protestantism, 1865–1915* (New Haven, 1940), pp. 174–78. James Dombrowski, *The Early Days of Christian Socialism in America* (New York, 1936), pp. 97–99. Roger E. Nelson, "A Study in Christian Socialism: William Dwight Porter Bliss," Master's Thesis, Episcopal Theological School, Cambridge, Mass., 1969. "The Social Conscience in American Churches," *The Commonwealth* (London), 32 (February, 1927): 41. Later Bliss acquired a house, known as the Wendell Phillips Union, which became the headquarters and meeting place for such organizations as the Central Labor Union, the Knights of Labor, the Anti-tenement House League, the Bricklayers' Union, and many others. Spencer Miller and Joseph Fletcher, *The Church and Industry* (New York, 1930), pp. 77–89. Chapter 5 gives the most detailed study of the Christian Social Union. The English group is discussed on pp. 17–25. See also Aaron Abell, *The Urban Impact on American Protestantism, 1865–1900* (Cambridge, Mass., 1943), pp. 107–08. *On Journey*, pp. 161–72.

12. Jessie Bernard, *Academic Women* (1964; rpt. New York, 1974), p. 5.

13. *On Journey*, pp. 181–84, 237–43, 256–68. Horace Scudder to Vida Scudder, May 1, 1900, Scudder Papers, WCA. There are also copies of her letters to the trustees as well as other letters in a file in WCA. See below Chapter 2, III "The 'Tainted Money' Controversy."

14. Miller and Fletcher, pp. 93–96. Hopkins, 243–44.

15. *On Journey*, pp. 185–89. Vida Scudder to President Ellen Pendleton, March 15, 1912, Scudder Papers, WCA.

16. *On Journey*, pp. 119–20, 377–90. Miller and Fletcher, p. 92. Winifred S. Hulbert, "The Prophetic Vision of Our Founders, II," SCHC Papers, 1955.

17. *On Journey*, p. 281. Reply to Herbert Barry's paper "Christianity

in International Relations" in *Papers and Addresses of the Thirty-third Church Congress (of the Protestant Episcopal Church) in the United States: Norfolk, Va., May 2–5, 1916,* (New York, 1916), p. 214. (Hereafter, *Papers and Addresses of the Thirty-third Church Congress.* "The Doubting Pacifist," *Yale Review* (N.S.) 6 (July, 1917):748. "What of the Church? . . . A Discussion," *The New World* 1, no. 4 (April, 1918):80. *On Journey,* pp. 279–86. See bibliography for other articles at this time.

18. *On Journey,* pp. 281, 298–302. *My Quest for Reality,* (Wellesley, 1952), p. 77.

19. Miller and Fletcher, p. 99. W. B. Spofford, "Talking It Over," *The Witness* 21, no. 5 (June 24, 1937):4–5.

20. As quoted in Alice Payne Hackett, *Wellesley, Part of the American Story* (New York, 1949), pp. 221–23.

21. Vida Scudder to Ellen Gates Starr, February 28, 1922, Ellen G. Starr Papers, SSC. *On Journey,* pp. 274, 292.

22. *On Journey,* pp. 304–06. "The Social Duty of Catholics," *American Church Monthly* 27 (May, 1930):335–42.

23. Joseph F. Fletcher, ed., *Christianity and Property* (Philadelphia: 1947), Dedication.

24. Personal letter to author from Douglas V. Steere, Haverford, Pa., March 12, 1976.

*Chapter Two*

1. See bibliography for a chronological list of articles.

2. *The Witness of Denial* (New York, 1895), Preface, also pp. 40–41. Scudder wrote often about her role as a teacher. For this period see "Influence and Independence" in *Andover Review,* 1890. Also *On Journey,* pp. 120–32.

3. *The Life of the Spirit in the Modern English Poets* (Boston, 1895), pp. 5–56 (hereafter cited as *The Life of the Spirit*). Reviewed in *Atlantic Monthly* 76 (July, 1895):130–34; *The Bookman* 1 (1895):342–43; *The Critic,* August 18, 1895, pp. 37–38; *The Dial* 19 (1895):97; *Poet Lore* 7 (1895):455–58. *On Journey,* pp. 127–30.

4. "The Greek Spirit in Shelley and Browning," Boston Browning Society, *Papers Selected to Represent the Work of the Society, 1886–1897* (New York, 1897), pp. 438–70.

5. *On Journey,* pp. 141–45. *College Settlements Association Report,*

*1893–94,* p. 43, SSC (hereafter *CSA Report*). The Denison House Records are at the Schlesinger Library in Cambridge.

6. "Social Ideals in English Letters: A Reading Course" in *Wellesley Alumnae Magazine* 11 (1926–27): 16–18, 70–73, 134–35, 202–03, 264–65, 358–59. *Social Ideals in English Letters* (Boston, 1898), pp. 2–5. For reviews of this book see *The Nation* 67 (December 22, 1898): 472–73; *Poet Lore* 11 (1899):418–25; *The New World* 8 (June, 1899):395–96.

7. "Christian Simplicity," SCHC Papers, 1896. "The Doubting Pacifist," *Yale Review,* 1917. See bibliography for details and for other articles on these topics.

8. As quoted by Winifred Hulbert in "Seventy-five Years of Progress in Social Justice," SCHC Papers, August 26, 1959.

9. *On Journey,* pp. 180–84. Letter of Horace Scudder to Vida Scudder, May 1, 1900, Scudder Papers, WCA. Here he gives detailed comments on the first draft of a letter she had prepared for trustees. A typed copy of the letter sent to trustees is in same location.

10. As quoted in Caro Lloyd, *Henry Demarest Lloyd: A Biography,* 2 vols. (New York: G. P. Putnam, 1912) 1:308.

11. An invitation to the conference is in the Scudder Papers in WCA. Also Conference Notes, p. 6, Brent Papers, Division of Manuscripts, Library of Congress.

12. "Ill-Gotten Gifts to Colleges," *Atlantic Monthly* 86 (November, 1890):679. *On Journey,* p. 181.

13. *On Journey,* p. 182. Henry D. Lloyd to Vida Scudder, June 19, 1900, Scudder Papers, WCA. Horace Scudder Diary (unpublished), April 26, 1900, and May 1, 1900, Horace Scudder Papers, Houghton Library, Cambridge, Mass.

*Chapter Three*

1. Vida Dutton Scudder to Jane Addams, Assisi, Umbria, April 27, 1902, The Jane Addams Papers, Swarthmore College Peace Collection (hereafter SCPC).

2. *A Listener in Babel* (Boston, 1903).

3. Horace Scudder to Vida Scudder, Chocorua, New Hampshire, July 19, 1901, Scudder Papers, WCA.

4. *A Listener in Babel,* pp. 42–43, 140–41. *On Journey,* p. 176.

5. Horace Scudder to Vida Scudder, Chocorua, New Hampshire, July 19, 1901, Scudder Papers, WCA.

6. Conference Notes. Brent Papers, Library of Congress.

7. *Saint Catherine of Siena as Seen in Her Letters.* (London, 1905), pp. 1–17. *On Journey*, pp. 241–48.

8. *On Journey*, p. 243.

9. *The Disciple of a Saint: Being the Imaginary Biography of Raniero di Landoccio dei Pagliaresi*, (London, 1907).

10. Vida D. Scudder to Anne Whitney, May 11, 1902, and November 27, 1904, Whitney Papers, WCA.

11. "A Hidden Weakness in Our Democracy," *Atlantic Monthly*, 89 (May, 1902):638–44.

12. "Democracy and Education," *Atlantic Monthly* 89 (June, 1902): 816–22.

13. "Democracy and Society," *Atlantic Monthly* 90 (September, 1902):348–54.

14. "Democracy and the Church," *Atlantic Monthly,* 90 (October, 1902):521–27.

15. *On Journey,* pp. 253–57. Also *CSA Report, 1903–1904*, pp. 32–33. Vida Scudder to Anne Whitney, March 4, 1904, Whitney Papers, WCA. Vida Scudder to Eva Channing, Wed. [March 6?], 1904, in Vida Scudder Papers, SSC. The poorer American and Irish neighbors that lived near Denison House in the early years had gradually been replaced by Syrians, Greeks, and Italians. Julia Ward Howe, Cornelia Warren, and Elizabeth Balch took an active interest in the Circolo Italo-Americano.

16. See Allen Davis, *Spearheads for Reform: The Social Settlements and the Progressive Movement, 1890–1914.* (New York, 1967), p. 89. Barbara Solomon, *Ancestors and Immigrants, A Changing New England Tradition* (1956; rpt. Chicago, 1972), pp. 143–45, 164–65.

17. *On Journey*, p. 257. *CSA Report, 1903–1904,* pp. 31–33. Solomon, pp. 81–151. See also John Higham, *Strangers in the Land* (1955; rpt. New York: 1963), for a survey of attitudes toward immigration restriction.

18. "The Irish Literary Drama," *Poet Lore* 16 (Spring, 1905):52.

19. "Experiments in Fellowship," *The Survey* 22 (April 3, 1909): 49–51.

*Chapter Four*

1. David A. Shannon, *The Socialist Party of America* (Chicago: Quadrangle, 1955), p. 61. Miller and Fletcher, pp. 93–96. Hopkins,

pp. 243–44. Founding members of the society also included Right Reverend Franklin S. Spalding of Utah, Rev. A. L. Byron-Curtiss, Right Reverend Benjamin Brewster, Bishop of Maine.

2. "The Church Socialist League," *The Churchman* 110 (August 8, 1914):183–84.

3. *Journal of the General Convention, 1910* (New York: Winthrop Press, 1910), Appendix 10, p. 538. In the report of this commission in the *Journal of the General Convention, 1913* Vida Scudder and Mary Simkhovitch are listed among the members. *The Church and the Hour: Reflections of a Socialist Churchwoman* (New York, 1917), p. 13.

4. "The Social Conscience of the Future, I," *Hibbert Journal* 7 (January, 1909):314–22. "The Social Conscience of the Future, II," *Hibbert Journal* 7 (April, 1909): 578–95. In *Hibbert Journal* 7 (July, 1909): 912–14, H. W. Inkpin, a socialist, took issue with Scudder's views in these articles, and she replied in *Hibbert Journal* 8 (October, 1909): 190–92. "Christianity in the Socialist State," *Hibbert Journal* 8 (April, 1910):562–81. "Religion and Socialism," *Harvard Theological Review* 3 (April, 1910): 230–47. "Socialism and Sacrifice," *Atlantic Monthly* 105 (June, 1910): 836–49. "Class Consciousness," *Atlantic Monthly* 107 (March, 1911): 320–30. "Forerunners," *Atlantic Monthly* 107 (August, 1911): 231–42.

5. Vida Scudder to Walter Rauschenbusch, September 21, [1912?], in Dores R. Sharpe Collection of Walter Rauschenbusch Papers, American Baptist Historical Society, Rochester, N.Y. Also *On Journey,* pp. 190–91.

6. *Socialism and Character* (Boston, 1912). *On Journey,* pp. 190–92. *An Introduction to the Writings of John Ruskin* (Boston, 1890). See her introduction to selection from "Unto This Last," p. 140, and Ruskin, p. 155.

7. Scudder frequently criticized the unions for not going beyond the immediate goal. She saw socialism as reconciling the two camps of employers and employees. See her address "Socialism as the Basis of Religious Unity" in *The Unity of Life: Proceedings of the National Federation of Religious Liberals,* ed. by H. W. Wilbur (Philadelphia, 1911), p. 70. See also *A Listener in Babel,* Chapter 9, "The Labor Leader," pp. 159–83.

8. This idea is strong in her address to women in the Lawrence Strike of 1912 quoted in *On Journey,* pp. 187–88.

9. Herbert Croly, *The Promise of American Life* (1909; rpt. New York: Capricorn Books, 1964), pp. 210–11.

10. Vida Scudder to Jane Addams, July 19, 1912, The Jane Addams Papers, SCPC. Vida Scudder to Walter Rauschenbusch, September 21, [1912?] and October 9, 1912, in Rauschenbusch Papers.

11. Walter Rauschenbusch, *Christianity and the Social Crisis* (New York: Macmillan, 1917) and *Christianizing the Social Order*, (New York, 1912). Josiah Royce was professor of philosophy at Harvard. See his *Philosophy of Loyalty* (New York: Macmillan, 1908). See W. R. Miller's brief introduction to Royce in *Contemporary American Protestant Thought: 1900–1970* (Indianapolis: Bobbs-Merrill, 1973), pp. 56–60, and Royce's "What is Vital to Christianity," pp. 60–99, reprinted in Miller from *Harvard Theological Review II*, 4 (October, 1909):408–45. *On Journey,* pp. 242–44, 333, 369.

## Chapter Five

1. "Miss Scudder's Criticized Speech: Just what she said at a Citizen's Meeting in Lawrence. . . ," *The Boston Common,* March 9, 1912, pp. 6–7. Clippings in Scudder Papers, WCA. Editorial from *Boston Evening Transcript,* March 5, 1912, was reprinted here. See also *Survey* 28 (April 16, 1912):76–79, and *Outlook* 100 (April 20, 1912): 846–47; *On Journey,* pp. 185–91; Hackett, pp. 184–87. Theresa Corcoran, "Vida Dutton Scudder and the Lawrence Textile Strike of 1912," *Essex Institute Historical Collections* 125 (July, 1979):183–95.

2. *On Journey,* p. 190. Vida Scudder to President Ellen Pendleton, March 15, 1912, Scudder Papers, WCA. Dr. Samuel B. Capen was president of the Wellesley College Board of Trustees at this time. For years he had supported the Immigration Restriction League. Solomon, pp. 84–88, 104, 106.

3. Vida Scudder to Walter Rauschenbusch, September 21, [1912] and October 9, 1912 in the Walter Rauschenbusch Papers.

4. Vida Scudder to Jane Addams, July 19, 1912, The Jane Addams Papers, SCPC. "Why Join the Party?" *Intercollegiate Socialist* 2 (October–November, 1913): 5. "Why Does Not the Church Turn Socialist," *The Coming Nation* (N.S.) 133 (March 29, 1913):9–10.

5. *The Church and the Hour* (New York, 1917), p. 1.

6. *Le Morte d'Arthur of Sir Thomas Malory* (1917; rpt. New York, 1965), pp. 307–8.

7. *Socialism and Character,* p. 171. "The Doubting Pacifist," *Yale Review* (N.S.) 6 (July, 1917): 740–42. Vida Scudder to Anne Whitney, Sunday, November 27, 1904, Whitney Papers, WCA. *On Journey,* pp. 281–88. "Socialists and the Problem of War" in *Intercollegiate Socialist* 5 (April–May, 1917): 20–21. In her autobiography Scudder admitted that her article "The Doubting Pacifist" was untimely although it did reflect her thinking in 1917. *On Journey,* p. 282. By 1937 she was a committed pacifist.

8. Reply to paper by Herbert Barry in *Papers and Addresses of the Thirty-third Church Congress,* 1916, p. 214.

9. "A Pacifist in Wartime" (1917?), clipping in the Scudder Papers, WCA, but title of publication taken from page head.

10. Helena Dudley to Jane Addams, August 7, 1918, The Jane Addams Papers, SCPC.

11. "What of the Church?—A Discussion," *New World* 1 (April, 1918):80. The *New World* was the organ of the Fellowship of Reconciliation. The title was changed to the *World Tomorrow* in June, 1918.

12. Vida Scudder to Emily G. Balch, September 1, 1919, as quoted in Mercedes Randall, *Improper Bostonian: Emily Greene Balch* (New York, 1964), pp. 252–53.

13. *Social Preparation for the Kingdom of God* 5 (April, 1918): 16–17. This was the newspaper of the Church Socialist League of which Jones was then President. George C. DeMille, *The Episcopal Church Since 1900* (New York, 1955), p. 165.

14. "Socialists and the Problem of War," *Intercollegiate Socialist,* April–May, 1917, p. 21. "Professor Scudder Not a Pacifist She Says," *Boston Globe,* January 26, 1919, clipping in Scudder Papers, WCA.

15. *On Journey,* p. 302. Scudder also joined the Women's International League for Peace and Freedom at this time.

16. *The Social Teachings of the Christian Year* (New York, 1921), pp. 7–8.

17. *On Journey,* pp. 304–6.

18. William B. Spofford, "Talking It Over," *Witness* 21 (June 24, 1937):405. Spofford was for many years executive secretary of the Church League for Industrial Democracy and editor of *Witness.* Scudder to J. M. Dent, April 25, 1919, in Dent Papers, London, England. In another letter of May 10, 1919, Scudder gave Dent a short personal account of the meeting and its prospects. Miller and Fletcher, *The*

*Church and Industry,* pp. 98–102. *Statement of Principles of the Church League for Industrial Democracy,* leaflet in Episcopal Library, 1 Joy Street, Boston, Mass. Also Scudder, "The Church League for Industrial Democracy," *The Church Militant* (March, 1923), p. 9. See also chapter 1 above.

19. *On Journey,* pp. 304–306.

*Chapter Six*

1. *On Journey,* pp. 240–41.

2. Vida Scudder to Ellen Gates Starr, February 26, 1922, Starr Papers, SSC. *Brother John* (Boston, 1927).

3. Evelyn Underhill pointed this out in her review in *The Spectator* 139 (December 27, 1928):1093–94. The reviews were favorable on the whole. See *Blackfriars* 9 (January, 1928):60–61; *Anglican Theological Review* 14 (Winter, 1932):90–91; *The Catholic World* 126 (November, 1927):277–78. *The Franciscan Adventure* (London, 1931), "The Lauds of Jacopone da Todi," pp. 332–53.

4. Ellen Gates Starr to Vida Dutton Scudder, Chicopee, Mass., June 16, 1927, Scudder Papers, SCHC Archives, Byfield, Mass.

5. Vida Scudder to Louise Manning Hodgkins, May 29, 1928, Scudder Papers, WCA.

6. *On Journey,* pp. 319–21.

7. As quoted in Hulbert, SCHC Papers, 1959. Vida Scudder to J. M. Dent, June 11, 1919, Dent Papers, London, England.

8. *The Franciscan Adventure,* Introduction, p. xvi, quoting Sabatier, "L'Originalité de S. François," *British Society of Franciscan Studies,* Extra Series 1, 1912: 6–7.

9. Ibid., 1:3; "Contrasts:" 29–32. "Privilege Unshared" is an expression that recurs often in Scudder and several times in *The Franciscan Adventure.* See here pp. 329, 351, 400.

10. *On Journey,* pp. 319–21.

11. Ibid., pp. 58–59. Father Dunstan, O.S.F.C., M.S., B. Litt. (Oxon), "Franciscan Poverty," *The Catholic World* 134 (February, 1932):529–37. C. [Father Cuthbert, O.S.F.C.] "St. Francis and Socialism," *The Tablet* (London), December 26, 1931. The review is signed C. A letter to Vida Scudder from Father Cuthbert, Assisi, December 8, 1931, referred to his review in *The Tablet* (letter in author's files). Reviewed also by Evelyn Underhill in *The Spectator,* November 21, 1931; George N. Shuster in *Commonweal,* February 3, 1932; Patrick J. Healey in

*Church History* 1 (June, 1932); Betty Drury in *New York Times Book Review,* December 6, 1931.

12. Rev. James Meyer, O.F.M., "Review of *The Franciscan Adventure*" in *Catholic Library World* 3, (May 15, 1932): 66. Excerpts from ten other reviews follow on pp. 66–67.

13. Reports of the Franciscan Institute held at Adelynrood, South Byfield, Mass., July 10–15, 1933, SCHC Papers. Fragments of correspondence between Scudder and Booth and others invited to the Institute are in the author's files.

14. Ibid. See the concluding pages of the report. The pages are not numbered.

15. *The Christian Attitude toward Private Property,* New Tracts for New Times, No. 11 (Milwaukee, 1934), p. 3. These are not new ideas for Scudder. See *Socialism and Character,* pp. 66–67, and *A Listener in Babel,* Ch. 10.

16. *Christian Citizenship,* pamphlet of a talk given to Woman's Auxiliary of the National Council (Atlantic City, 1934), pp. 4–5.

17. Review of Ralph M. Huber, O.F.M. Conv., *A Documented History of the Franciscan Order, 1182–1517.* (Milwaukee: The Nowing Publishing Apostolate, 1944) in *Franciscan Studies* 6 (March, 1946): 93–99. Letters to Scudder from Kilian Lynch, O.F.M., St. Bonaventure, N. Y., November 1, November 6, and December 3, 1945, in author's file.

18. Joseph F. Fletcher, ed., *Christianity and Property* (Philadelphia, 1947), Dedication. Scudder's "Anglican Thought on Property" is Chapter 6, pp. 124–50.

*Chapter Seven*

1. *On Journey,* pp. 9–12, 431–33. "Journal III," 1934–35, SSC.

2. "The Privilege of Age," *Atlantic Monthly* 151 (February, 1933):205–11.

3. *Father Huntington, Founder of the Order of the Holy Cross,* (New York, 1940).

4. Father Allen Whittemore to Vida Scudder, West Park, N.Y., October 9, 1939, in the James O. S. Huntington Papers, Archives of the Order of the Holy Cross, West Park, N.Y. Whittemore mentioned specific pages in the book where he took issue with Scudder's interpretations.

5. Henry George, author of *Progress and Poverty* (New York:

Lovell Company, 1879), was a popular lecturer and social critic who had great influence in the Protestant churches in the late nineteenth century. Huntington was one of many young clergymen who supported Henry George in his campaign for mayor of New York City in 1886. Father McGlynn was a Roman Catholic priest who was excommunicated for his political views and activities, then later reinstated in his church. *Father Huntington*, p. 139.

6. See note 4. Also Ellen Gates Starr to Vida Scudder, Chicopee, Mass., June 16, 1927, Scudder Papers, SCHC Archives.

7. Paul A. Carter, *The Decline and Revival of the Social Gospel* (1956; rpt. Hamden, Conn., 1971), p. 13. Henry May, *Protestant Churches and Industrial America*, pp. 240–41. For another more recent and comprehensive study see Donald B. Meyer, *The Protestant Search for Political Realism, 1919–1941.* (Berkeley, 1960).

8. *Father Huntington*, pp. 177, 227, 257, 284. "Footnote on Father Huntington," *Living Church* 103 (April 2, 1941): 11. "Father Huntington" Letter to the Editor in *Living Church* 102 (December 18, 1940):2.

9. May, p. 241.

10. James Arthur Muller, "Father Huntington and the Beginnings of Religious Orders for Men in the Episcopal Church: A Review," in *Historical Magazine of the Protestant Episcopal Church* 10 (December, 1941): 312–29.

11. In the archives of the Order of the Holy Cross are many letters and reminiscences of Father Huntington which could document or substantiate the spirit Scudder wanted to convey on pages 177, 212, 219, for example.

*Chapter Eight*

1. *The Privilege of Age: Essays Spiritual and Secular.* (New York, 1939).

2. Jones spoke of Scudder as the "original leader" of this group. Rufus Jones to Vida Scudder, Haverford College, October 14, 1947, Scudder Papers, SCHC Archives. The leaders in the revival of the Anglican Social Movement in England in the 1930s published a journal, *Christendom,* hence the appellation, the Christendom group. Scudder was one of the American associate editors and in close touch with the Anglo-Catholic School of Social Studies at Oxford. A. V. Demant, Maurice Reckitt, and W. G. Peck were in the English

group. In a personal interview with Mother Pattie Ellis, C.W.C., in Buffalo, New York, May, 1972, Ellis spoke of the encouragement Scudder had given her. See her editorial "Vida D. Scudder" in *Work and Way* 1 (October, 1953):1, the newsletter of the community (Scudder Papers, WCA). There is some interesting correspondence between Smyth and Scudder in the Archives of the Society of the Catholic Commonwealth, Prince William, New Brunswick, Canada.

3. Vida Scudder to Anne Whitney, November 27, 1904, Whitney Papers, WCA.

4. See *Papers and Addresses of the Thirty-third Church Congress,* pp. 168–69, 213–15 for Scudder's replies. Scudder's address was reprinted in *Yale Review* and in her *The Church and the Hour.* See bibliography.

5. *On Journey,* pp. 302–04, 334.

6. "The Discipline of Wartime," *Unity* (November 6, 1939), p. 72. *On Journey,* p. 337.

7. "Foemen Vassals: A Pacifist Apologia," *Protestant* 4 (October–November, 1941): 45–46.

8. *My Quest for Reality,* pp. 73–77. See her note added to p. 77.

9. Barbara Welter, "The Cult of True Womanhood," *American Quarterly* 18 (Summer, 1966): 151–74.

10. *On Journey,* pp. 58, 65–67.

11. *Christian Union* 35 (April, 1887). See bibliography for details of the series.

12. *Poet Lore* 1 (October 15, 1889):449–65.

13. *Relation of College Women to the Social Need,* Association of Collegiate Alumnae, Series 11, no. 3, (n.p., 1891), p. 5.

14. "Woman and Socialism," *Yale Review* (N.S.), 3 (April, 1914): 454.

15. "Women and the Present Crisis," *The Social Preparation for the Kingdom of God* (November, 1914), p. 76.

16. *Listener in Babel,* pp. 267–69.

17. As quoted by Fletcher in *Christianity and Property,* Dedication. Quotation is from William Morris's *A Dream of John Ball.* In an interview with the Reverend Joseph Fletcher he often referred to Scudder as "Aunt Vida." See also letters signed "M. V." or "Mother Vida" in Scudder Papers, SCHC Archives and also letters in author's files.

18. *On Journey,* Part II, Ch. 7, pp. 217–28. This entire chapter deals

with friendship on various levels and especially friendships among women.

19. Clara French, *Class Prophecy, Class of '84*, pamphlet in SSC. *On Journey,* pp. 61–74.

20. "Influence and Independence." *Andover Review* 13 (February, 1890) : 167.

21. *On Journey,* pp. 119–20. See letters of Scudder to Mary Mc-Dermott, archives of the Community of the Way of the Cross, Buffalo, N. Y. Also Scudder letters in SCHC Archives and in WCA. *On Journey,* pp. 377–90; Part III, Ch. 6, "A House of Holiness" is about the Society of the Companions of the Holy Cross.

22. Vida Scudder to Ellen Gates Starr, Wellesley, Mass., June 16, 1922, Starr Papers, SSC.

23. Florence Converse, *Diana Victrix* (New York: Houghton-Mifflin, 1897). Converse died February, 1967. See also Nan Bauer Maglin, "Vida to Florence: 'Comrade and Companion'", *Frontiers* 4 (Spring, 1979) : 13–19.

24. Florence Converse, *The Burden of Christopher* (New York: Houghton Mifflin, 1900).

25. The handwritten poem is inscribed "F.C. to V.D.S., V.D.S. to F.C., S.C.H.C." and may have been written jointly by the two friends. The poem may have been published anonymously earlier, but the first published version located is in the *Collected Poems of Florence Converse* (London: J. M. Dent, 1937), under the dedication "To Vida Dutton Scudder."

# Selected Bibliography

## PRIMARY SOURCES

Most of Vida Dutton Scudder's personal papers have been lost but interesting pieces of correspondence continue to turn up in other collections. These are given in references when used in this study. The most useful Scudder materials are in the Wellesley College Archives, in the Sophia Smith Collection, Smith College, in the Archives of the Society of the Companions of the Holy Cross, Byfield, Massachusetts. There are interesting Scudder letters in the Archives of the Community of the Way of the Cross, Buffalo, N.Y., in the archives of the Society of the Catholic Commonwealth, Prince William, New Brunswick, and in the Dent Papers, London, England. The Denison House Records, 1892–1960 are in the Schlesinger Library, Cambridge, Mass., and the College Settlements Association Records are in the Sophia Smith Collection. The Bishop Charles Brent Papers are in the Library of Congress. Wellesley College has a bibliography prepared by Florence Converse and a detailed bibliography by Peter Oliver. The bibliography in my dissertation on Scudder is the most complete. Since this is the first book on Scudder, the following bibliography will include her major published articles.

## 1. Books

*Brother John: A Tale of the First Franciscans.* Boston: Little, Brown, 1927.

*The Church and the Hour. Reflections of a Socialist Churchwoman.* New York: E. P. Dutton and Co., 1917.

*The Disciple of a Saint: Being the Imaginary Biography of Raniero di Landoccio dei Pagliaresi.* London: J. M. Dent and Co., 1907.

*Father Huntington: Founder of the Order of the Holy Cross.* New York: E. P. Dutton and Co., 1940.

*The Franciscan Adventure: A Study of the First Hundred Years of the Order of St. Francis of Assisi.* London: J. M. Dent and Co., 1931.

*Introduction to the Study of English Literature.* New York: Globe School Book Co., 1901.

*The Life of the Spirit in the Modern English Poets.* Boston: Houghton, Mifflin and Co., 1895.

*A Listener in Babel: Being a Series of Imaginary Conversations.* Boston: Houghton, Mifflin and Co., 1903.

*Le Morte d'Arthur of Sir Thomas Malory and Its Sources.* London, 1917; rpt. New York: Haskell House, 1965.

*My Quest for Reality.* Wellesley: By the Author, 1952. At the North Country Press, Saint Albans, Vermont.

*On Journey.* New York: E. P. Dutton and Co., 1937.

*The Privilege of Age: Essays Spiritual and Secular.* New York: E. P. Dutton and Co., 1939.

*Saint Catherine of Siena as Seen in Her Letters.* London: J. M. Dent and Co., 1905.

*Social Ideals in English Letters.* Boston: Houghton, Mifflin and Co., 1898.

*The Social Teachings of the Christian Year: Lectures Delivered at the Cambridge (Massachusetts) Conference.* New York: E. P. Dutton and Co., 1921.

*Socialism and Character.* Boston: Houghton, Mifflin and Co., 1912.

*The Witness of Denial.* New York: E. P. Dutton and Co., 1895.


2. Books edited or with introduction by Vida D. Scudder

*A Church Year-Book of Social Justice.* New York: E. P. Dutton and Co., 1919.

*The Ecclesiastical History of the English Nation.* Everyman's Library. London: J. M. Dent and Sons, 1910.

*George MacDonald: Poems.* With C. F. [Clara French] New York: E. P. Dutton and Co., 1887.

*Jesus and Politics* by Harold B. Shepheard. New York: E. P. Dutton and Co., 1915.

*The Journal with Other Writings of John Woolman.* Everyman's Library. London: J. M. Dent and Sons, 1910.

*Introduction to the Writings of John Ruskin.* The Students' Series of English Classics. Boston: Leach, Shewell and Sanborn, 1890.

*Letters to Her Companions* by Emily Malbone Morgan with a bio-

graphical sketch by Emily Sophie Brown. The Society of the
Companions of the Holy Cross: South Byfield, Mass., 1944.

*Macaulay's Essay on Lord Clive.* The Students' Series of English Classics.
Boston: Leach, Shewell and Sanborn, 1889.

*Old Chester Tales.* New York: Harper and Bros., 1898.

*Prometheus Unbound.* Boston: D. C. Heath, 1892.

*Shorter English Poems.* New York: Scott, Foresman and Co., 1912.


3. Selected Essays and Pamphlets (in chronological order)

"Père Antoine." *The Atlantic Monthly* 52 (October, 1883): 498–503.
(Published under pseudonym of Davida Coit.)

"Immortality and Evolution." *The New Englander* 7 (September,
1884): 707–17.

"Lake of the Poets." *Outlook* 51 (January 19, 1885): 96–97.

"The Poetic Element in Medieval Drama." *The Atlantic Monthly* 56
(September, 1885): 407–15. (Published under pseudonym of
Davida Coit).

"Work for Women at Oxford." *The Christian Union* 33 (April 29,
1886): 7–8, and (May 6, 1886), 9–10.

*The Grotesque in Gothic Art,* n.p., 1887.

"The Moral Dangers of Musical Devotees." *The Andover Review* 7
(January, 1887): 46–53.

"The Effect on Character of a College Education: I." *The Christian
Union* 35 (April 7, 1887): 12.

"The Effect on Character of a College Education: II." *The Christian
Union* 35, (April 14, 1887): 12.

"The Educated Woman as a Social Factor: III." *The Christian Union*
35 (April 21, 1887): 12–13.

"A Protest." *The Christian Union* 35, no. 24 (June 16, 1887): 16.

"The Effect of the Scientific Temper on Modern Poetry." *The Andover
Review* 8 (September, 1887): 225–46.

"The Effect of the Scientific Temper on Modern Poetry. (Concluded)." *The Andover Review* 8 (October, 1887): 351–66.

"A Shadow of Gold." *The Overland Monthly,* October 1887, pp.
380–89.

*Mitsu-Yu Nissi; or the Japanese Wedding* by V.D.S. and F.M.B.
[Frona M. Brooks]. Young's Standard Series of Plays. Boston: H. A.
Young and Co., 1888.

"The Poetry of Matthew Arnold." *The Andover Review* 10 (September, 1888): 232–49.

"A Flight in the Dark." By S.K. [Sophia Kirk] and V.D.S. *The Atlantic Monthly* 62 (December, 1888): 766–77.

"A New Departure in Philanthropy." *The Christian Union* 37 (May 10, 1888): 588–89; (May 17, 1888): 620–21.

"The Curate's Afterthought." *The Christian Union* 39 (January 17, 1889): 74–75; (January 24, 1889): 106–07.

"Womanhood and Modern Poetry." *Poet Lore* 1 (October 15, 1889): 449–65.

"Influence and Independence." By S.K. [Sophia Kirk] and V.D.S. *The Andover Review* 13 (February, 1890): 167–81.

"The College Settlement in New York City." *The Dawn* 2 (October, 1890): 230–33.

*The Relation of College Women to Social Need.* Publication of the Association of Collegiate Alumnae, Series 2, no. 3, n.p., 1891.

"Socialism and Spiritual Progress—A Speculation." An address delivered before the Society of Christian Socialists, Boston, March, 1891. *The Andover Review* 16 (July, 1891): 49–67. Reprinted as pamphlet by the Church Social Union. Series A, January 1, 1896.

"A Modern Legend." *Harper's Magazine* 82 (January, 1891: 300–03.

"A Comparative Study of Wordsworth's 'Michael,' Tennyson's 'Enoch Arden,' Browning's 'Andrea del Sarto.'" *Poet Lore* 3 (February 16, 1891): 87–93.

"Wulfy: a Waif: A Christmas Sketch from Life." *The Century* 43 (December, 1891): 276–80.

"The Place of College Settlements." *The Andover Review* 18 (October, 1892): 339–50.

"A Glimpse into Life." *The Wellesley Magazine* 1 (February 18, 1893): 221–32.

"College Settlements." *The Holy Cross Magazine* 5 (January, 1894): 37–38.

"Two Italian Poets." *The Wellesley Magazine* 3 (January 12, 1895): 185–88.

"College Settlements and Religion." *The Congregationalist* 80 (May 2, 1895): 682.

"Denison House." First in series of papers by the Society of the Companions of the Holy Cross, June, 1895.

"Alfred de Vigny." *The Wellesley Magazine* 4 (May 16, 1896):
    421–28.

"Notes from Denison House." *Smith College Monthly* 3, no. 6 (March,
    1896): 42–43.

"The Greek Spirit in Shelley and Browning." Boston Browning Society,
    *Papers Selected to Represent the Work of the Society from 1886–
    1897.* New York and London: Macmillan, 1897, pp. 438–70.

*Christian Simplicity.* A publication of the Christian Social Union, No.
    52, August 15, 1898. Boston, Office of the Secretary, 1 Joy St.,
    1898. A rewriting of the 1896 SCHC Paper of the same title.

"Arnold as an Abiding Force." *The Dial* 27 (December 16, 1899):
    481–82.

"The College Woman and Social Reform." *Celebration of the Quarter-
    Centenary of Smith College, October Second and Third, 1900.*
    Cambridge: Riverside Press, 1900.

"The College Settlements Movement." *Smith College Monthly,* May,
    1900, pp. 447–54.

"Recollections of Ruskin." The Contributors' Club, *The Atlantic
    Monthly* 85 (April, 1900): 568–71.

"Ill-Gotten Gifts to Colleges." *The Atlantic Monthly* 86 (November,
    1900): 675–79.

"The Mosaics at Ravenna." *The Churchman* 85 (April 12, 1902):
    462–65.

"A Hidden Weakness in Our Democracy." *The Atlantic Monthly* 89
    (May, 1902): 638–44.

"College Settlements and College Women." *Outlook* 70 (April 19,
    1902): 973–76.

"Democracy and Education." *The Atlantic Monthly* 89 (June, 1902):
    816–22.

"The Shrine of the Narcissus." *The Churchman* 86 (August 23, 1902):
    220–21.

"Democracy and Society." *The Atlantic Monthly* 90 (September,
    1902): 348–54.

"Democracy and the Church." *The Atlantic Monthly* 90 (October,
    1902): 521–27.

"The Educational Element in Dante's Divine Comedy, I." *The Kinder-
    garten Review* 13 (November, 1902): 127–35.

"The Educational Element in Dante's Divine Comedy, II." *The Kinder-
    garten Review* 13 (December, 1902).

"The Uses of Poetry." *A Glad New Year.* A publication of Department of English Literature, Wellesley College, 1902, pp. 1–10.

"Sicilian Holy Days." *The Churchman* 87 (April 11, 1903): 485–88, 491.

"Footprints of St. Francis." *The Outlook* 74 (June 6, 1903): 332–38.

"The Heart of the Alps." *The Churchman* 88 (October 3, 1903): 391–95.

"Modern Innocents Abroad." *Smith College Monthly,* November, 1903, pp. 112–14.

"Wayfaring Memories." *Persephone and Other Poems by the Members of the English Literature Department, Wellesley College.* Boston: The Fort Hill Press, 1905, pp. 135–62.

"The Irish Literary Drama." *Poet Lore* 16 (March, 1905): 40–53.

"Denison House and the Italians." *Chicago Commons* 10 (May, 1905): 287–90.

"The Social Conscience of the Future: I." *The Hibbert Journal* 7 (January, 1909): 314–22. Part II, *The Hibbert Journal* 7 (April, 1909): 578–95.

"Ten Years Later." *The Jabberwock,* February, 1909. Magazine of Girls' Latin School, Boston. Clipping in Scudder Papers, WCA.

"Experiments in Fellowship." *The Survey* 22 (April 3, 1909): 47–51.

"The Social Conscience of the Future." *The Hibbert Journal* 8 (October, 1909): 190–92. (Reply to H. W. Inkpin's rejoinder to her article in the Discussion Column of *The Hibbert Journal*).

"Christianity in the Socialist State." *The Hibbert Journal* 8 (April, 1910): 562–81.

"Religion and Socialism." *The Harvard Theological Review* 3 (April, 1910): 230–47.

"Socialism and Sacrifice." *The Atlantic Monthly* 105 (June, 1910): 836–49.

"Cathedral Tower." *Chatauqua* 61 (December, 1910): 86–87.

"Socialism as the Basis of Religious Unity." *The Unity of Life. Proceedings and Papers of the National Federation of Religious Liberals Held in New York, April 26–28, 1911.* Edited by Henry W. Wilbur. Philadelphia: The Federation, 1911.

"Class Consciousness." *The Atlantic Monthly* 107 (March, 1911): 320–30.

"Forerunners." *The Atlantic Monthly* 107 (August, 1911): 231–42.

"A Settlement Opportunity." *The Wellesley College News* 20, no. 18 (February 15, 1912): 1.

"Miss Scudder's Criticized Speech: Just What She Said at a Citizens' Meeting in Lawrence, to which exception has been so excitedly taken by the Brahmins." *The Boston Common*, March 9, 1912, pp. 6–7. Reprinted in *The Outlook* 100 (April 20, 1912): 846–47.

"For Justice' Sake." *The Survey* 28 (April 16, 1912): 76–79.

"On Magic Casements." *The Century Magazine* 85 (December, 1912): 316–18.

"Aliens' Fine Qualities." Letter to editor. *Boston Globe,* March 17, 1912.

"The Moral Assets of the Class Struggle: Address of Miss Vida D. Scudder at the Ford Hall Meeting, January 12, 1913." *Ford Hall Folks* 1, no. 4 (January 19, 1913): 2–6.

"More Abundant Life." *Life and Labor* 3, no. 3 (March, 1913): 1.

"An Awakening in New England." *Everyman* 24 (March 28, 1913): 742.

"Why Doesn't the Church Turn Socialist?" *The Coming Nation* (N.S.), 133, (March 29, 1913): 9–10.

"Why Join the Party?" *The Intercollegiate Socialist* 2 (October-November, 1913): 5–7.

"The Church's Great Opportunity." *The Churchman* 109 (February 21, 1914): 235–36, 248.

"Masefield and Gibson: A Renaissance in Social Poetry." *The Survey* 31 (March 7, 1914): 707–09.

"Woman and Socialism." *The Yale Review* (N.S.) 3 (April, 1914): 454–70.

"The Passing of College Hall, Wellesley." *The Churchman* 109 (April 4, 1914): 434–36.

"The Church Socialist League." *The Churchman* 110 (August 8, 1914): 183–84.

"Some Pointed Questions on the Ethics of Property." *The Churchman* 110 (September 19, 1914): 473.

"Women and the Present Crisis." *The Social Preparation for the Kingdom of God*, November, 1914, pp. 76–77.

"Some Signs of Hope." *The Intercollegiate Socialist* 3 (April–May, 1915): 6–8.

"Religious Life." *The Wellesley College News* 23 (April, 1915): 39–40.

"Plato as a Novelist." *The Yale Review* (N.S.) 4 (July, 1915): 788–804.

Letter to the editor. *The Masses* 8, No. 2 (December, 1915): 21. Reprinted in her *The Church and the Hour*.

"The Ethics of Socialism." Address given at Labor Day Weekend Conference by Vida Dutton Scudder. Quoted by Harry Laidler in "Jottings from the Conference Notebook" in *Intercollegiate Socialist* 4 (October–November, 1915): 14–20.

"The Alleged Failure of the Church to Meet the Social Emergency." *Papers and Addresses of the Thirty-third Church Congress* (of the Protestant Episcopal Church) *in the United States: Norfolk, Va. May 2–5, 1916.* New York: Edwin S. Gorham, 1916, pp. 133–53. Reprinted in *The Yale Review* (N.S.), 6 (January, 1917): 326–41 and in her *The Church and The Hour*.

Letter to the editor. *The Masses* 8, no. 4 (February, 1916): 20. Reprinted in her *The Church and the Hour*.

"Academic Freedom." *The Century Magazine* 92 (June, 1916): 222–30.

"A Plea for Social Intercession." *The Churchman* 115 (January 6, 1917): 9–10. Reprinted in *The Church and the Hour*.

"Strength, Song, Salvation." *The Churchman* 115 (March 17, 1917): 293–94.

"The Doubting Pacifist." *Yale Review* (N.S.) 6 (July, 1917): 738–51. Reprinted in The Privilege of Age.

Editorial. *The Social Preparation for the Kingdom of God* 4 (October, 1917): 12–14.

"A Christmas Message." *The Churchman* 116 (December 22, 1917): 804–05.

"Remarks of Chairman of Session of Intercollegiate Socialist Society Annual Convention, December, 1916." As quoted by Harry Laidler in "Jottings from the I.S.S. Convention" in *Intercollegiate Socialist* 5, (February–March, 1917): 14–15.

"Socialists and the Problem of War: A Symposium." *Intercollegiate Socialist* 5, (April–May, 1917):7, 20–21.

"A Pacifist in War Time." [1917?], p. 10. Clipping in Scudder Papers in Wellesley College Archives.

Editorial. *The Social Preparation for the Kingdom of God* 5, (July, 1918): 12–13.

"How Draw Workingmen to Church?" *The American Church Monthly* 4 (September, 1918): 26:35.

"What of the Church?—A Discussion." *The New World* 1, (April, 1918): 79–81.

"Bishop Jones & Reaction on the Church." Letter to the editor, *The Churchman* 117 (January 12, 1918): 65.

"Prophecy Coming True." *The Social Preparation for the Kingdom of God* 5 (January, 1919): 12–14.

"The Social Teachings of the Church Year." *Anglican Theological Review* 1 (March, 1919): 383–406.

"The Church Today." *Anglican Theological Review* 2, (October, 1919): 106–13.

"Seed-vessel Time." *The Atlantic Monthly* 124 (November, 1919): 717–20. Reprinted in The Privilege of Age.

"Almost Too Good to Be True." *The World Tomorrow* 2, (December, 1919): 323–25.

"The Socialist Review." *The Socialist Review* 8: (December, 1919), 48–49.

"Pacifism-Prof. Scudder's Denial of this Title." *Boston Globe,* January 26, 1919. Clipping in Scudder Papers in Wellesley College Archives.

"Beyond Stewardship." *The Living Church* 62, no. 3, (November 15, 1919): 77–78.

"The Church and the League of Nations." *The World Tomorrow* 2, (February, 1919): 54.

"The Strike in Lawrence." *The Christian Register* 98, no. 18 (May, 1919): 416–18.

"On Being a Stockholder." *The New Republic* 23 (July 14, 1920): 198–200.

"The New Chivalry." *The Venturer*, October, 1920, pp. 31–36.

"Education for the New Day." *The World Tomorrow* 3 (December, 1920): 355–58.

"John Woolman Today." *The Friend* 93 (March, 1920): 434–37.

"Is the Christian Church Christian? From Another Point of View." *The Christian Century* 38, (April 7, 1921): 11–14.

"What Is Luxury?" *The World Tomorrow* 5 (June, 1922): 163–64. Reprinted in The Privilege of Age.

"Fear Not." *The Social Preparation for the Kingdom of God* 9 (July/October, 1922): 8–9.

"Property and Creative Joy." *The Christian Century* 41 (November 9, 1922): 1392–94.

"Franciscan Parallels." *Anglican Theological Review* 5 (March, 1923): 282–98.

"The Church League for Industrial Democracy." *The Church Militant*, March, 1923, p. 9.

"Christian Motives and Economic Reform." *The Congregationalist* 108, no. 27 (July 5, 1923): 8–9.

"The Last Beatitude." *The Witness*, February, 1923, pp. 7–8.

"Christianity: Conservative or Revolutionary." *The World Tomorrow* 7 (August, 1924): 244–45.

"The College Girl's Mind." *The New Republic* 40 (October 1, 1924): 123–24. Reprinted in The Privilege of Age.

"Christianity in the Next Fifty Years." *The Western Christian Advocate*, January 15, 1925. (In Scudder Papers in Wellesley College Archives.)

"Forerunners of the C.L.I.D.: Our Heritage from the Past." *The Witness*, 9 (September 24, 1925).

"Why the Saints?" *The Commonweal* 3 (December 9, 1925): 127–29.

"A Modern Saint of the Fourteenth Century: A Non-Catholic Appreciation of St. Catherine." *Rosary Magazine* 48 (April, 1926): 1–6.

"The Bishops' Crusade to Stir Our Wills to Action." *The Witness* 11, no. 22 (January 20, 1927): 3–4.

"The Social Conscience in American Churches." *The Commonwealth* (London) 32 (February, 1927): 41–44.

"Sons of Francis. What Is Their Legacy?" *The Churchman* 125, no. 10 (March 5, 1927): 16–17.

"Brother John: Monk and Friar." *The Churchman* 135, no. 14 (April 2, 1927): 12–14. From her *Brother John*. (Other selections from this book in nos. 15, 17, 18).

"Forever Arriving." A contribution to the symposium entitled "Why Utopias Never Come." *The Adult Bible Class Magazine*, June, 1927, pp. 258–59.

"The Privileges of a College Teacher." *The Wellesley Alumnae Magazine* 11 (August, 1927): 327–29.

"A Pedagogic Sunset." *The Atlantic Monthly* 141 (June, 1928): 781–91. Reprinted in The Privilege of Age.

"The Larks of St. Francis." *The World Tomorrow* 11 (December, 1928): 503–04. Reprinted in The Privilege of Age.

"The Federal Council of Churches. A Report." *The Witness* 13, no. 19 (December 27, 1928): 3–4.

"The Franciscan Studies Summer School at Oxford." *The Tablet,* August 18, 1928, pp. 215–17.

"A Wandering Mind In Italy." *The Wellesley College Literary Review,* January, 1929, pp. 3–7.

"Mysticism and Social Passion." *The World Tomorrow* 13 (March, 1930): 122–25. Reprinted in The Privilege of Age.

"Adventuring for God." *The Congregationalist* 115 (April 24, 1930): 549, 558.

"The Social Duty of Catholics." *The American Church Monthly* 27 (May, 1930): 335–42.

"The Franciscan Adventure." *The Atlantic Monthly* 145 (June, 1930): 808–19.

"Can the Church Be Saved?" *The Christian Century* 58 (January 21, 1931): 82–85.

"The Waiting Task." *Christendom* (London) 1 (June, 1931): 121–28.

"The Church and Industry." *The Witness* 16 (September 24, 1931): 8–9.

"Thanksgiving and Hard Times. If You Were President How Would You Proclaim Thanksgiving Day?" *The Christian Century* 48 (November 18, 1931): 1457. Reprinted in Privilege of Age.

"The Christian Way Out." *The Witness* 16, no. 27 (February 25, 1932): 4–5.

"Christian and Churchwoman: Why?" *The Living Church* 87 (August 13, 1932): 355.

"St. Francis and Today." *The C.S.S. Review* (Christa Seva Sangha Ashram, Poona, India) 2 (October, 1932): 279–83.

"The Privilege of Age." *The Atlantic Monthly* 151 (February, 1933): 205–11. Reprinted in The Privilege of Age.

"A Franciscan Episode." *The Churchman* 147, no. 19 (August 15, 1933): 16–17.

"The Next Hundred Years of the Catholic Revival: II. Alternatives and Opportunities." *Christendom* (London) III (September, 1933): 190–99. Reprinted in Privilege of Age.

"A Franciscan Institute." *The Commonweal* 18 (September 1, 1933):
427–28.

"The Cross in Utopia." *The Hibbert Journal* 32 (October, 1933):
56–69.

*The Christian Attitude toward Private Property*. New Tracts for New
Times. Milwaukee, Wisc.: Morehouse Publishing Co., 1934. Reprinted in Privilege of Age.

"Social Problems Facing the Church in 1934." *The Spirit of Missions*
99 (January, 1934): 6–9. Reprinted as: *The Church and Social
Justice*. New York: The National Council, Department of Christian Social Service, 1934.

"Christian Conflicts." *Christendom* (London) 4, no. 3 (March, 1934):
12–23.

"The Anglo-Catholic Movement in the Next Century: Its Social Outlook." *The Living Church* 90 (March 10, 1934): 589–91.

*Christian Citizenship. Presented at the Triennial Meeting of The
Woman's Auxiliary of the National Council, Atlantic City, New Jersey.*
New York: Woman's Auxiliary, 1934.

"St. Catherine of Siena." *The Holy Cross Magazine*, April, 1934, pp.
147–50.

"St. Bonaventure." *The Holy Cross Magazine*, July, 1934, pp. 147–50.

"A Conference of the Eastern Church." *The Living Church* 91 (August
11, 1934): 213.

"St. Francis of Assisi." *The Holy Cross Magazine*, October, 1934, pp.
219–34.

"Promise and Problem." *The Living Church* 91 (November 17, 1934):
619–20.

"Work." *The Hibbert Journal* 33 (July, 1935): 498–510. Reprinted
in Privilege of Age.

"Varieties of Christian Experience." *The Holy Cross Magazine*, January, 1937, pp. 17–19.

"A Little Tour in the Mind of Lenin." *The Christian Century* 54
(March 24, 1937): 379–82. Reprinted in Privilege of Age.

"The Art of Corporate Worship." A review of *Worship* by Evelyn
Underhill. *Christendom* (Chicago) 2 (Summer, 1937): 376–87.
Reprinted in Privilege of Age.

"C.L.I.D. at General Convention." Letter to the editor. *The Living
Church* 97 (September 25, 1937): 358–59.

"Now! Now!" *The Living Church* 98 (January 19, 1938): 73–74.

"Price of Liberty." *The Commonweal* 27 (April 15, 1938): 680–82.

"Prophetic Elements in the Franciscan Movement." *Christendom* (Chicago) 3 (Summer, 1938): 378–90.

"Conflicting Loyalties." *Radical Religion* 3 (Winter, 1938): 9–12.

"The United Front." *The Living Church* 100 (January 4, 1939): 15–16. Reprinted in the *Protestant Digest* I (March, 1939): 42–47.

"The Discipline of Wartime." *Unity,* November 6, 1939.

"The Cross Eternal: I." *Holy Cross Magazine,* September, 1940, pp. 226–29.

"The Cross Eternal: II." *Holy Cross Magazine,* October, 1940, pp. 296–99.

"Father Huntington." *The Living Church* 102, no. 4 (December 18, 1940): 2.

Untitled contribution to "1941—Their Pacifism Holds." *Fellowship,* January, 1941. Clipping in Scudder Papers, Wellesley College Archives.

"The Significance of Malvern for American Churchmen." *The Living Church* 103, no. 8 (March 5, 1941): 13–14.

"Consummation." *The Witness* 25, no. 3 (March 27, 1941): 3–4.

"Footnote on Father Huntington." *The Living Church* 103, no. 11 (April 2, 1941): 11.

"The War and God's Judgement." *The Living Church* 103, no. 13 (April 16, 1941): 10–11.

"Foemen Vassals: A Pacifist Apologia." *The Protestant* 4, no. 2 (October–November, 1941): 45–54.

"Know Your Classics." *The Witness* 25, no. 34 (December 4, 1941): 3.

"Messages from Malvern." *The Witness* 25 (November 6, 1941): 7–9.

"Denison House, a Community Center for Real Democracy." *Denison House Herald* 8, no. 5 (December, 1941): 1.

"The Confessions of St. Augustine." *The Witness* 25, no. 38 (January 8, 1942): 9.

"The Rule of St. Benedict." *The Witness* 25, no. 42 (February 5, 1942): 10.

"The Dream of the Rood." *The Witness* 25, no. 46 (March 5, 1942): 9.

"The Book of St. Bernard on the Love of God." *The Witness* 25, no. 49 (March 26, 1942): 10.

"Malvern 1941." *The Living Church* 104, no. 24 (June 14, 1942): 10–11.

"Franciscan Leaven." *The Friend* (Philadelphia) 117 (Eleventh Month, 1943): 147–49.

Untitled contribution to "Free Speech for Fascists. Eleven Distinguished Men and Women Answer a Question Vital to the Times." *New Masses,* January 11, 1944. Clipping in Scudder Papers, Wellesley College Archives.

Untitled contribution to "My Vote and Why: A Symposium on the Presidential Campaign." *New Masses* 53, no. 2 (October 10, 1944): 10.

"The Church Holds the Key to Peace." *Forth,* November, 1944, p. 7.

"Jerusalem, Not Geneva." Letter to the editor. *The Christian Century* 62 (January 17, 1945): 82–83.

"John Woolman: Precursor." *The Witness* 28 (April 5, 1945): 8–9.

"The Secret Work of Grace: A Whitsuntide Meditation." *The Holy Cross Magazine,* May, 1945, pp. 141–42.

"William Blake: Christian Revolutionist." *The Witness* 28 (May 17, 1945): 7–8.

"Frustration: A Note of Cheer." *Saturday Review of Literature* 28 (November 17, 1945): 60.

"How to Pray in These Difficult Days." *The Church Woman,* June, 1946, pp. 5–8.

"Raphael M. Huber. A Documented History of the Franciscan Order, 1182–1517." *Franciscan Studies* 6 (March, 1946): 93–99.

"Social Rebirth. First of a Series on Social Rebirth." *The Witness* 30, no. 37 (October 16, 1947): 11–12. Other essays on the topic appeared in next seven issues of *The Witness.*

"Anglican Thought on Property." *Christianity and Property.* Edited by Joseph F. Fletcher. Philadelphia: The Westminster Press, 1947, pp. 124–50.

## SECONDARY SOURCES

There are no lengthy studies of Vida Scudder or her works. The following are the sources most useful for an understanding of the groups and movements with which Scudder was concerned.

## 1. Books

Abell, Aaron. *The Urban Impact on American Protestantism 1865–1900.* Cambridge: Harvard University Press, 1943. A detailed study of the work of churches in industrial areas with good analysis of Social Gospel.

Bernard Jessie. *Academic Women.* 1964; rpt. New York: New American Library, 1974. Sociological study by a woman academic highlighting pioneers in higher education of women. Singles out Scudder as one of leading academic women of time.

Carter, Paul A. *The Decline and Revival of the Social Gospel.* 1956; rpt. Hamden, Conn.: Archon, 1971. An excellent account of social and political issues facing the churches in the twentieth century. Little reference to Scudder but last chapter discusses impact of war on the pacifist principle and consequently on the Social Gospel.

Davis, Allen. *Spearheads for Reform: The Social Settlements and the Progressive Movement, 1890–1914.* New York: Oxford University Press, 1967. This catches the spirit of the early settlement workers and Scudder's role in the movement.

DeMille, George C. *The Episcopal Church Since 1900.* New York: Morehouse-Gorham, 1955. A useful survey of the Episcopal Church but little reference to left-wing movements in that Church.

Dilling, Elizabeth. *The Red Network: A Who's Who Handbook of Radicals for Patriots.* By the author, 1934. Useful to trace interaction of many of the radical church organizations.

Dombrowski, James. *The Early Days of Christian Socialism in America.* New York: Columbia University Press, 1936. Important pioneer study of Christian Socialism in America and the other radical movements in American churches.

Fletcher, Joseph F., ed. *Christianity and Property.* Philadelphia: Westminster Press, 1947.

Gabriel, Ralph H. *The Course of American Democratic Thought.* New York: Ronald Press, 1940. Important survey of intellectual developments in the United States with special section on changes in American Protestantism.

Hackett, Alice Payne. *Wellesley, Part of the American Story.* New York: E. P. Dutton, 1949. Superseded the Converse history of Wellesley. Important for background of Scudder's academic milieu.

Higham, John. *Strangers in the Land.* 1955; rpt. New York: Atheneum,

1963. Examines patterns of nativism in the United States. Appreciative look at efforts of the settlement workers with new immigrants.

Hopkins, Charles Howard. *The Rise of the Social Gospel in American Protestantism, 1865–1915.* New Haven: Yale University Press, 1940. Most scholarly and most interesting account of Social Gospel. Several references to Scudder's role in early movements in the Episcopal Church.

Jones, Peter d'A. *The Christian Socialist Revival, 1877–1914.* Princeton: Princeton University Press, 1968. Comprehensive study of Christian Socialist movement in various churches in England and of the influence of these on similar movements in churches in the United States.

Mann, Arthur. *Yankee Reformers in an Urban Age.* Cambridge: Harvard University Press, 1954. Examines social reform in days when Boston was in vanguard of such movements. Readable, reliable, and essential to understanding the milieu in which Scudder came of age. Mann highlighted Scudder in one chapter on newer women. His chapter on Robert Woods provides an interesting contrast between these two reformers.

May, Henry. *Protestant Churches and Industrial America.* 1949; rpt. New York: Octagon Books, 1963. Surveys the same period as Hopkins' but looks at variety of expressions of social Christianity and stresses importance of these movements to progressive reform. Refers to Scudder.

Meyer, Donald B. *The Protestant Search for Political Realism, 1919–1941.* Berkeley: University of California Press, 1960. Detailed scholarly study of crises of religion in inter-war years and impact of these years of social concern on religion itself.

Miller, Spencer, Jr., and Joseph F. Fletcher. *The Church and Industry.* New York: Longmans, Green and Co., 1930. Includes sections on such groups as Society of Companions of Holy Cross, and Church Association for Advancement of Interests of Labor not found elsewhere.

Mott, Frank Luther. *A History of American Magazines.* 5 vols. Cambridge: Belknap Press of Harvard University Press, 1968. Surveys American magazines from the mid-eighteenth century to the early twentieth century. Essential for study of Scudder who wrote for so many and such varied radical groups.

O'Neill, William L. *Everyone Was Brave.* Chicago: Quadrangle Books, 1969. A lively interpretative history of American feminism stressing the failure of the women to forge an ideology. O'Neill singles out Scudder as one of the ten leaders.

Quint, Howard H. *The Forging of American Socialism.* New York: Bobbs-Merrill Co. Inc., 1953. A good history of American socialist movements in the 1890s.

Randall, Mercedes. *Improper Bostonian: Emily Green Balch.* New York: Twayne Publishers, 1964. As a colleague of Scudder at Wellesley, in the settlement, and in Church reform, Balch is an important source of information about Scudder and her work.

Rauschenbusch, Walter. *Christianizing the Social Order.* New York: Macmillan Co., 1912. Scudder was very much influenced by the work of Rauschenbusch and he also asked her to read several of his manuscripts. Scudder would have liked him to come out directly for socialism but he declined.

Rideout, Walter B. *The Radical Novel in the United States, 1900–1954.* Cambridge: Harvard University Press, 1956. The only book that discusses Scudder as a literary figure. Considers *A Listener in Babel* as one of the early protest novels but does not consider its importance for radical feminism.

Sabatier, Paul. *Vie de Saint François d'Assise.* 4th ed. Paris: Fischbacher, 1894. Scudder was greatly influenced by Sabatier and was instrumental in having the Boston Public Library secure his Franciscan collection after his death. Her own later Franciscan studies benefitted from the acquisition.

Solomon, Barbara Miller. *Ancestors and Immigrants: A Changing New England Tradition.* 1956; rpt. Chicago: University of Chicago Press, 1972. Interesting study of the intellectual exercise of the Brahmins at the turn of the century in shaping their attitudes to the immigrants. Several references to Scudder here.

Weinstein, James. *The Decline of Socialism in America, 1912–1925.* New York: Random House, 1967. Excellent recent study of socialism covering the years when Scudder was most involved in the Socialist Party.

2. Articles and Dissertations

Corcoran, Theresa. *Vida Dutton Scudder: The Progressive Years.* Ph.D. dissertation, Georgetown University, 1973.

————. "Vida Dutton Scudder: The Impact of World War I on the Radical Woman Professor." *Anglican Theological Review,* Spring, 1975, pp. 164–181. Shows the diverging opinions of many of the women reformers and academics and the changing attitudes toward pacifism.

————. "Vida Dutton Scudder and the Lawrence Textile Strike of 1912." *Essex Institute Historical Collections* 125 (July, 1979): 183–195. Focuses on Scudder's address to workers in Lawrence and of her speech and on the repercussions in Boston and Wellesley.

Frederick, Peter J. "Vida Dutton Scudder: The Professor As Social Activist." *The New England Quarterly* 43 (September, 1970): 407–33. The only lengthy study of Scudder. Appreciative and interestingly written survey. Relies largely on her *On Journey.*

Muller, James Arthur. "*Father Huntington* and the Beginnings of Religious Orders For Men In the Episcopal Church." *The Historical Magazines of Protestant Episcopal Church* 10 (December, 1941): 312–329. Review of Scudder's book.

Maglin, Nan Bauer. "Vida to Florence: 'Comrade and Companion,'" *Frontiers* 4 (Fall, 1979): 13–20. Perceptive analysis of relation between Scudder and Converse from their published writings.

# Index

144